Knowing
Jesus
Knowing *God*

by David Marshall

*'This book is all about Jesus.
It has given me a whole new basis
for my faith.'*

Bible Versions

The Bible versions used are identified by the following initials:

NIV New International Version.
(Copyright 1979 and 1984 International Bible Society) – used throughout
except where expressed by the following versions.

TNIV Today's New International Version.
(Copyright 2006 Zondervan. Study Bible.)

NLT New Living Translation, second edition.
(Copyright 2008 Tyndale House Publishers. Study Bible.)

ESV English Standard Version, Anglicised edition. (Copyright 2002 Collins.)

NRSV New Revised Standard Version. (Copyright 1989 Thomas Nelson.)

MGE The Message: The Bible in Contemporary Language.
(Copyright 2002 NavPress.)

KJV King James Version.

Author's italics used throughout.

Printed 2014.
Reprinted 2014.
Copyright © 2014
Autumn House Publications (Europe) Ltd

British Library Cataloguing in Publication Data.
A catalogue record for this book is available from the British Library.

ISBN 978-1-907244-54-4
Published by Autumn House Publications (Europe) Ltd,
Grantham, Lincolnshire.

Designed by Abigail Murphy.

Printed in China.

Knowing
Jesus
Knowing *God*

by David Marshall

*'This book is all about Jesus.
It has given me a whole new basis
for my faith.'*

Knowing Jesus Knowing God

Contents

Contents

Knowing *Jesus* Knowing *God*

Upfront

In search of the Author . . .

It's years since we first sent a man into space. When he returned he reported to the world's press that he had not found God there.

C. S. Lewis responded that it was as if Hamlet, Prince of Denmark, had gone up into the attic of his castle and reported back that he had not found Shakespeare there.

God is not an object in His own universe to be put in a lab and analysed.

Rather, God relates to us more as a playwright relates to the characters in his play. We – the characters in the play – must examine the evidence the Playwright has left in His play.

The God of the Bible is not a man in the attic. He is the Playwright. We find Him by the clues to His reality that He has written into His universe, including us.

A playwright can only be known through personal revelation: what evidence about himself he has left in the play.

The most important evidence for the existence of God is Jesus

Upfront

Christ. The Playwright did more than leak a few hints about Himself in the text. He gave Himself the central role.

The Playwright makes a personal appearance in the play – as the main character!

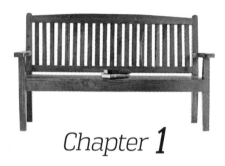

Chapter *1*

The Bottom Line About God

'Get to the point!'
'What's the bottom line?'
'Let's cut to the chase!'

These have become well-worn phrases in our generation-in-a-hurry.

Meaning much the same thing, someone recently said, 'Let's choke the chicken!' That made me smile, but may have ruffled the chicken!

Not long ago, a young-man-in-a-hurry combined two clichés together when he asked me the question:

'Is there "a fast track" to "the bottom line" – *about God*?'

That sparked all sorts of thought-currents.

If such a bottom line about God existed, where would it be?

In the Bible, surely. But can the Bible be said to have a 'fast track' to 'the bottom line' about God?

The Bible is not so much a book as a library of books. Collectively they represent God's revelation of Himself to man. But

The Bottom Line About God

can they be said to have a 'fast track' to 'the bottom line' of God's self-revelation?

I didn't find the fast track until I realised what the Bible's bottom line is.

When I found the bottom line it was after years of study. The words in which I expressed that bottom line, however, were words which I had been given towards the beginning of my journey.

I was one of eight young people permitted to ask a no-advanced-warning question to a great Christian scholar in the sixties.

Since I was given a 'one question with no supplementaries' stipulation, I had to choose a cut-to-the-chase question.

The question I chose was one that – years earlier – had been addressed to Karl Barth, another great Christian scholar.

Barth was asked to define the bottom line of Christian belief. To the amusement of his enemies and (at first) the bafflement of his friends, Barth replied in the words of a familiar children's hymn: *'Jesus loves me! This I know, for the Bible tells me so'* (originally by Anna Warner).

There was widespread laughter in Karl Barth's audience – that ended in embarrassment when everyone looked at the scholar's face and saw that he was entirely serious.

In the absence of a better question, years after it had been asked of Karl Barth, I asked it of Michael Ramsey,[1] my celebrity scholar. It came towards the end of the question-and-answer session. I was the last of the eight young people permitted to ask a question, and the only questioner not expecting to become a clergyman. To my mind the earlier questions the Archbishop grappled with had been somewhat obscure. Certainly they failed to provoke stimulating answers.

When I asked my 'What is the bottom line of Christian belief?' question, the ample Archbish smiled broadly for the first time. Was he pitying the ignorance of his shy interrogator, or was he

Knowing **Jesus** *Knowing* **God**

finally beginning to enjoy himself? A bit of both, perhaps.

'A good question,' he said, becoming almost animated.

He then gave me his answer. At the time I did not fully appreciate the validity of what he said. That took years.

'The bottom line?' he queried. 'It is this. God is Christlike. In God there is no unChristlikeness at all. And if you think there is, it is because you have misunderstood something; because Jesus is the perfect revelation of God.'

That, I have come to believe, is the bottom line of the Bible's revelation of God.

Is there a 'fast track' to it?

[1] The 100th Archbishop of Canterbury.

Chapter 2

The Fast Track to God

Mark's Gospel hits the ground running. This is, says Mark, 'the gospel about Jesus Christ, the Son of God' (Mark 1:1).

John's Gospel, too, gets to the point right away. Its opening statements are certainly among the most profound in all literature:

'In the beginning was the Word, and the Word was with God, and the Word was God. He was with God in the beginning. Through him all things were made; without him nothing was made that has been made' (John 1:1-3).

John wrote his Gospel in Ephesus. He did so after many decades' experience of communicating the Christian Gospel to the Greek world. Those who preached the Christian Gospel to Jewish communities had the task of proving that Jesus was the Messiah from the Old Testament Scripture. To Greek communities, like the one in Ephesus, the word *Messiah* meant nothing. Communicators of the Gospel to the Greco-Roman world had a tougher job to do. The opening of John's Gospel is especially brilliant because it makes it clear that John found a

Knowing *Jesus* Knowing **God**

concept that Jews and Greeks had in common: the *logos*, or the Word.

The Greeks knew that the Word was the agent of creation. John identified the Word with Jesus, the Christ or Messiah. The Word, like the Messiah, was with God, was God, and had been inseparable from God for eternity past.

John is saying: Jesus came not only to show us what God *was* like or *is* like. He came to show us what God *has always been like*.

Our Father God never changes (James 1:17). With the Father, 'Jesus Christ is the same yesterday and today and for ever' (Hebrews 13:8).

The fast track to God's character is to look at the life and character of Jesus.

Jesus is the perfect revelation of God. There is nothing unJesus-like in God. Never has been. Hence the fast track to knowing God is to know Jesus. Whereas Jesus is present through the Bible, the four Gospels – Matthew, Mark, Luke and John – are where His life and character come over with crystal clarity. If there is one part of Scripture where God is most supremely accessible, it is in the four Gospels of the New Testament.

While we encounter God through Jesus in the Gospels, encountering Him is not the same as *knowing* Him. To know Him we must enter into a relationship with Him. The Gospels cannot be bettered as the point of primary encounter with God, or as the source of the clearest revelation of God. Nevertheless, because God *is* – and is like Jesus – we must enter into a relationship with Him. That involves not just the Gospels, where God is revealed, but encountering and relating to the living God through prayer. It also involves embracing the Gospel (Good News) revealed in all of the Bible. The fact is that the four Gospels that recount the life, ministry, character, death and resurrection of Jesus are not just primary historical sources with regard to God. They are the accounts of the events which, when they are embraced, make

The Fast Track to God

possible new and everlasting life. In a word: *salvation*.

The fast track we are looking for is the way to salvation.

In one sense, therefore, the Gospels are the means to an end.

Chapter *3*

The Gospels

Is one of the four Gospels – Matthew, Mark, Luke and John – better at revealing God than the others?

Here I must make a confession. My favourite Gospel is the one I happen to be studying at any given time. Please bear with me.

Matthew. I can make a case for Matthew. From a very early time, Christians always put Matthew's Gospel first. Not because it was written first. It quotes Mark, so it cannot have been written first. But Matthew is the Gospel writer who reveals Jesus as the fulfilment of all the Messianic hopes of the Old Testament. That gives Matthew's Gospel a wonderful Jewish flavour, and makes it an ideal bridging book between the Old and New Testaments that make up the Bible.

In Matthew's Gospel Jesus has much to say about the Jewish law and Jewish teaching. His encounters with the Jewish authorities are also detailed. Most importantly, Matthew's Gospel gives the most column inches to Jesus' own teachings.

Matthew is indispensable.

The Gospels

Luke. The case for Luke's indispensability almost makes itself. Bible authorities often introduce their commentaries on Luke's Gospel by describing it as 'the best life of Christ ever written'. My background as an editor and historian inclines me to agree with them. Of all the Gospel writers, Luke is most conscientious with his sources and most comprehensive in his coverage of the Jesus story. He is at pains, also, to link the principal events of Jesus' life with the key political leaders alive at that time.

Luke rises above the prejudices of his culture and generation by taking care to provide detail on the role women played in the life and mission of Jesus.

Luke's is the Gospel for the underdog: not just the 'slumdog', but those on the far edges of society for reasons other than poverty. Luke's Gospel shows Jesus as the Friend of 'outcasts' and 'sinners'.

Luke wants us to known that 'the love of God is broader than the measure of man's mind'. The third Gospel would also be indispensable if only because it is the only Gospel to include the Parable of the Lost Son.

John. Having said all that, I must risk baffling the reader by stating that the Gospel that really moves mountains for me is the Gospel of John! Yet John omits the birth of Jesus, his baptism, the temptations, the Gethsemane experience, and the ascension. He also omits the parables.

For all that, John mainlines the very mind of God.

John's closeness to Jesus meant that he had special knowledge. One of the consequences of this is that disciples like Thomas, Andrew, Judas and Philip are more than just bit-part players in the fourth Gospel. His additional details mean that they have real supporting roles.

Although John omits certain important events, he includes others that the other Gospel writers omit. He includes the Cana wedding, perhaps to remind us that Jesus changes the water of our lives into wine every single day. He details the Nicodemus visit, because it was to that professor of theology that Jesus expounded the core of the Christian Gospel: new birth. The woman of Samaria was given full coverage, because John wants us to know that Jesus reaches over every high wall of separation when He offers the water of life. Gender, race, track record, historical baggage: none of these are a hindrance to His grace.

It is fair to say that John wrote his Gospel some thirty years after Matthew, Mark and Luke wrote theirs. John knew what had been 'covered elsewhere' – and what had not.

Mark. In an age of haste and hurry, we cannot miss out Mark's Gospel. Mark is a major source for Matthew and Luke, who were so confident of his accuracy that they quoted him *verbatim*.

Mark's Gospel has all the characteristics of an authentic, eyewitness account. It is a primary historical source. But who was the eyewitness? Not Mark.

In the second century both Papias of Phrygia and Iranaeus of Lyons identified Mark as the man who had been the secretary and interpreter of the disciple Peter. In the third century Tertullian of Carthage and Eusebius of Caesarea said the same thing. Even without their testimony, we would be obliged to note that nothing happens in Mark for which Peter is not present. It is an eyewitness account. Mark's is a fast-paced Gospel. He covers the salient points in just sixteen chapters.

Jesus is the Central Figure in Scripture, and I believe it is legitimate to state that all of Scripture should be viewed through the lenses of the four Gospels that most clearly reveal Him.

But is Jesus clearly revealed in sources outside of the Gospels? Even outside of Scripture?

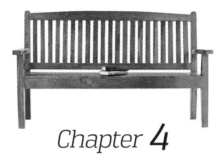

Chapter 4

The Fifth Gospel

The Gospel according to – whom?

Postmodern people – the folks who live near you – respect, and regard as authentic, a Gospel other than Mark and the rest.

At the heart of Christianity is a miracle. Jesus told Nicodemus about it in John's Gospel, chapter three. Paul, the great champion of Christ and His resurrection, often wrote about it. Here is one example of the sort of thing he said: 'Therefore, if anyone is in Christ, he is a new creation; the old has gone, the new has come!' (2 Corinthians 5:17.)

Non-Christians are apt to look for evidence that that is still true. The question they ask about Christianity is, 'Does it work?' If they find evidence that it does, *then* they will consider checking out Matthew, Mark, Luke and John – even exploring the claims of Christ.

My mother gave me my first Bible. At the back of it, broadcaster and evangelist H. M. S. Richards had written some Bible background and guidelines as to how best to study the Bible. He

Knowing *Jesus* Knowing **God**

had also quoted an 'Author Unknown' poem which ended with the lines, *'The only Gospel that some men will read, Is the Gospel according to you.'* Perhaps aware that, though an eager student, I needed to follow more closely the Life revealed in those Gospels, my mother handwrote those lines on the flyleaf of the Bible before signing 'Mother'.

That's the sort of thing that gets to you.

It also *stays* with you.

For fifty years – even after that Bible had fallen to pieces and Mother had fallen into her last sleep – it vexed me. It seemed to me that it placed too much responsibility on my shoulders. It was asking too much of me. Surely, I would tell myself, my friends and my family, we are saved solely by God's grace and the gift of faith that He gives us. We are not saved by track record or performance. All true, of course. For that is the substance of those wonderful gist verses in Ephesians 2:8, 9:

'For by grace you have been saved through faith. And this is not your own doing; it is the gift of God, not a result of works, so that no one may boast' (ESV).

But that crystal-clear Gospel summary is followed by another verse (vs. 10, TNIV): 'For we are God's handiwork, created in Christ Jesus to do good works . . .'

Hence, while there is only one perfect Example, Jesus Christ, people are entitled to look for some sort of reflection of that Example in me. They are entitled to check whether there is evidence that, by being 'created anew in Christ Jesus', there is anything of Christ Jesus in the way I live. *Do* I mirror Jesus? If it hasn't made any difference in my life, might they reach the conclusion that the miracle doesn't work any more?

Postmoderns are looking for evidence that the miracle at the heart of Christianity still happens.

Presuming to speak for his class, one student once said to me:
'You've told us about William Wilberforce and his long

The Fifth Gospel

campaign to get first the slave trade, then slavery itself, abolished; and you've demonstrated that what fired him up and kept him fired up was his Christianity . . .

'You've demonstrated that what drove Elizabeth Fry's lifelong campaign to improve prison conditions was her Christianity . . .

'You've shown us that the amazing contribution Anthony Ashley Cooper, Earl of Shaftesbury, made to improving the lot of children and working hours and conditions in factories and mines was down to his strong Christian commitment . . .

'Heck! You've even convinced us that the whole British reform movement – Earl Grey to Gladstone, Lloyd George to Aneurin Bevan – 'owed more to Methodism than to Marx' . . .

'But all those guys and gals have been dead for generations. *Aren't we due some more up-to-date evidence that Christianity still works?*'

His (or their) point was valid.

The snag is, of course, this. Even if you see the ideals of Jesus reflected in the lives of Wilberforce, Shaftesbury, *and so on* – the reflection falls a long way short of a reflection of Jesus. Nevertheless, if their cases are accepted as evidence that Christianity works, and even if we can produce 'more up-to-date evidence', the greatest Example of all is still the One that shines out of Matthew, Mark, Luke and John, and it is by looking to Him that the Spirit 'makes us more and more like him' (2 Corinthians 3:18, NLT). But, based on that promise, should those of us who have been examining Jesus, the perfect revelation of God, begin to be a bit like Him?

We're not necessarily talking sainthood, here. Mother Teresa was a marvellous person, but not many of us are like her. That's what vexed me for years about the handwritten exhortation of my mother. I thought she was looking for too exact a replica of Jesus in me. It would be great if it happened. But it hasn't so far.

Mother was just reminding me of that wonderful 'P.S.' to Paul's exposition of the Gospel provided in the general epistle of James (2:14-26). If we bring Paul's and James's teachings together, we hear something like this: 'We are saved by faith alone, but not by a faith that remains alone. True faith will always produce a changed life.'

Grace makes us gracious.

Graciousness produces lives committed to service for others, and totally sensitive to the feelings of others. Christians should spend not only their money but themselves.

If you were arrested for being a Christian, would they find enough evidence to convict you?

If the answer is 'Yes', postmoderns are far more likely to decide that your case is valid.

Take the cases of Joanie and Jay. . . .

You? Me? Seriously?

Chapter 5

You? Me? Seriously?

Jay lived in the United States, where, over the summer, Christian youth attend church-run camps. As a boy he had so thoroughly enjoyed those camps that he looked forward to them all year. By the time he was 24 he had enjoyed the entire age range of camps, and, though looking forward to the annual family camp now that he was married, when the summer came round he really missed those youth camps.

It was then that church authorities appointed Jay Senior Counsellor at the camp that catered for late-teen youth. They also arranged a number of training courses for him.

When Jay was in his sixties he was still working as a youth camp counsellor! Over the years he had dealt with most kinds of problems. Whenever camp counsellors encountered a particularly knotty problem or situation, they took it to Jay. That was how, late one night, Jay came to be introduced to Joanie. Joanie had been, by turns, angry and sullen and was clearly 'having a difficult time'. The counsellors left it to Jay to uncover the root problem. So that

Knowing *Jesus* Knowing *God*

Joanie felt that she had some support, her female counsellor remained with her as Jay sought to discover the nature of that problem.

From Joanie's vocab it was clear to Jay that she had come to camp from a non-Christian background. It turned out that a large congregation had, from the previous year, employed Joanie, then 18, as church cleaner. When summer came they had given her the opportunity to attend camp and had offered to pay for her to do so. Joanie had taken them up on their offer and, after what amounted to a series of misunderstandings, there she was, in sullen-mode, with her counsellor and Jay.

Joanie's story, once it got started, took a long time in the telling. Neither Jay nor the female counsellor were prepared for its heartbreaking nature.

Joanie had been sexually abused by her father from the age of 4. As she poured out the story, two things became obvious to Jay. First, that Joanie had never told her story to anyone before. Second, that she carried a huge sense of guilt, mistakenly believing herself partly responsible for her father's actions.

Joanie's wrists were scarred. Jay invited her to tell him what happened.

'I tried to kill myself,' said Joanie, as if stating the obvious.

Jay's next question was asked to ascertain whether Joanie's suicide attempts had been cries for help: 'Was there a reason why you didn't go through with it?'

What Joanie had said thus far was of great interest to social services and the police. They were on the scene first light the following day. Jay and the female counsellor sat on either side of Joanie when her father was sentenced ten months later.

It was Joanie's answer to the suicide question that especially absorbed Jay's attention when he reviewed that night's harrowing revelations. It was the only light that had shone thus far. Asked if there was a reason why she had not gone through with the

You? Me? Seriously?

suicide, Joanie cryptically replied: 'Well. I got to thinking. We have this youth pastor at our church. . . .' (She used the expression 'our church' she had heard the church members use.)

Jay experienced a sharp intake of breath. For an instant he was preparing himself for another ugly story of abuse. None came.

Joanie went on, 'He was not long married when he first came. I had watched him ever since he arrived. . . .' It became clear that Joanie had taken the opportunity to attend both mid-week and weekend services. These, she later indicated, had been experienced as a 'mixed blessing'. She had witnessed some of the symptoms of 'churchianity'. The youth pastor and his young wife who, unbeknown to themselves, had been absorbing Joanie's attention, were just about the only shaft of light she had seen.

'I watched the youth pastor squeeze his wife in the lunch queue *when he was sure no one was looking*,' said Joanie. 'Even in church,' she went on, 'they had a special way of looking at one another. Sometimes they hug, *when they are sure no one is looking*. . . .' That phrase again!

Joanie explained that, on days when there were no services, she would watch members of the pastoral team go to and from their offices to the car park. 'One day, I was looking out of a church window to the car park. The youth pastor was walking with his wife out to the car. Theirs was the only car there. Nobody was around. That man walked all the way round the car, opened the door, and waited until she got in. Then he walked all the way back round the car and got in himself . . . *and there was nobody even looking!*'

At that point Jay was a bit fogged. He could not see the connection between Joanie's story of the abuse she had suffered and the suicide she had attempted, and the youth pastor's courtesy to his wife. In the end Jay said so. Do *you* see the connection?

Knowing *Jesus* Knowing *God*

'Well,' Joanie blurted out with impatience, 'I got to thinking. Not all men are like my dad.'

'You're right,' Jay began, 'Not all men are like your father. . . .'

Joanie interrupted Jay as if she had not heard the comment. 'Jay, do you think that youth pastor is a Christian?'

'More than an outside chance,' said Jay, who knew all the pastors from their days at camp. 'What's his name?'

Joanie told him.

'An "outside chance" did I say?' asked Jay. 'It's a racing certainty!'

'Right!' said Joanie triumphantly. 'That's why I'm here. *I* want to be a Christian!'

Why did she want to be a Christian?

She had seen a young man being affectionate and respectful to his wife – and this was crucial – when he thought no one was looking.

That's the power of a little detail from a consistently-lived Christian life.

Influenza is not just the name of a nasty virus; it's the Italian word for *influence*. English tourists returned from Italy in 1750 with the symptoms of a cold accompanied by a high fever. They made it clear to their physician that they had caught it from Italians. 'What were the Italians calling it?' he asked.

'They kept talking about *influenza di freddo* [the influence of the cold],' the patients responded. And the name stuck.

All of us are, by nature, contagious people. Our example tends to spread to others at least as easily as the flu.

We, in turn, unconsciously imitate the patterns of behaviour that please or impress us. We reflect the characters we most admire.

More can be taught by example in one week than by a lifetime of talk.

You? Me? Seriously?

'You are writing a Gospel, a chapter each day,
By the deeds that you do, by the words that you say.
Men read what you write, whether faithless or true.
Say, what is the Gospel according to you?'[1]
    Author unknown

The best way to be a living Gospel is –
- To read the Jesus story in one or more of the four Gospels;
- To find out from them and from other parts of the New Testament what the Good News is;
- To embrace the Good News.

Having encountered Jesus in the Gospels and come to know Him, we need to find out –
- What the story means;
- And how to get into it.

We need to be part of the narrative.

For that to happen, our reading of the Gospels must be accompanied by prayer to the Person who is at their centre.

'Beloved, we are God's children now, and what we will be has not yet appeared; but we know that when he appears we shall be like him, because we shall see him as he is.' 1 John 3:2, ESV.

We begin to be like Jesus as we read His story in the Gospels and encounter Him through prayer.

For the people down your street, the 'fast track' to 'the bottom line about God' is apt to be the extent to which Jesus' life is reflected in yours. You could call that, 'The Gospel According to You'.

---

[1] *http://hjortland.blogspot.co.uk/2009/09/gospel-according-to-you*

Chapter 6

'A Religious Man'

Exposure to the Gospels and prayer are vitally important in getting to know God and grasping His Good News. Religion doesn't always help.

This is what religion sounds like:

'Give me just a fiver's worth of God, please. No more. Nothing radical. I'm choosing a feel-good faith. I don't want my comfort zone invaded. Certainly none of this New Birth stuff. Give me the warmth of the womb. Not New Birth and the growing pains that come afterwards.

'Just a fiver's worth of God. You understand? And not the flesh-and-blood God revealed in Jesus. He would be bound to invade my comfort zone. I don't want a living, breathing God. I want a Christmas Christ I can keep in the crib all year with a dummy in His mouth to stop His noise.

'Now, don't get me wrong. I can take a few rules and a bit of ritual. But nothing that interferes with my quality of life. . . .'

'A Religious Man'

Is that a gross caricature of contemporary religion or 'churchianity' these days? Yes, perhaps. But it's not a *total* caricature of religion in any age.

Notice the word *religion*. We are talking religion here. What makes Christianity unique is that it is the only world faith that is *not* a religion!

What *is* religion? The bottom line of any definition is bound to be along these lines:

religion, noun. *1. the belief in and worship of a God or gods. 2. a system which binds the believer to rules, regulations and ritual as a means of achieving salvation.*

origin. Latin. religio. 'obligation'.

The god in whom religious people believe is custom-made, bespoke, made-to-measure. A god on their own terms. God-in-a-box. Strictly man-made.

Almost from the start there have been people who have wanted to neuter or tame Christianity. Two great twentieth-century Christian writers used the word *churchianity* to describe this neutered form. They were C. S. Lewis and Walter Martin.

Let's look at an extreme case that illustrates why – as Lewis and Martin observed – we must beware of the

fiver's worth of god-in-a-box

\+

rules

\+

rituals

= churchianity.

If the name Alistair Cooke rings bells with you, the chances are you are thinking of a cricketer. However, if you are of a 'certain age' there's a slim chance that you have in mind a man with a nasal, Anglo-American accent who spoke on BBC Radio 4 between 1946 and 2004, and did so for fifteen minutes every

Knowing *Jesus* Knowing **God**

week. If that is your Alistair Cooke, then you have been privileged to have heard, though not necessarily seen, the greatest journalist of his century.

Alistair Cooke presented his *Letter from America* for most of my lifetime. I tried never to miss it. He interpreted the politics, people and culture of the USA for his British listeners. He was always at his best when analysing the life and contribution of the great Americans of the past. In the pre-internet age, I so much enjoyed one of his analyses that I wrote and told him so. Within the week I received a handwritten reply, together with a photocopy of the typescript of his broadcast. He began his bio of a prominent American with the words of the widow of the deceased following the funeral.

'My married life was like one long, unclouded honeymoon,' she had said. 'He did everything to make me happy. He gave me his wholehearted devotion. I had love, home and contentment.'

During the broadcast Cooke had paused after reading those words, before saying, 'What a fellow.'

The prominent American in question, it appeared, had been a non-smoker and non-drinker. He did not gamble. Abstemious in his eating habits, he was a vegetarian. He loved animals. He was deeply suspicious of stimulants. Tea, coffee and cola were in the no-no category. He did not use profane language, and used every means he could to discourage it within hearing distance. He never showed an interest in any women other than his wife. He was a model father.

Neighbours of his said that you could set your clock by him. At 8.50 every morning he was seen on his doorstep, fondly embracing his wife. He would then be seen walking the three blocks to his office.

After a ten-hour day, he walked home. Supper came next. Evenings were usually spent at home, though he and his wife occasionally went out to a classical concert.

'A Religious Man'

He died of a heart attack at 75.

Cooke could not resist another, 'What a man!' and 'No wonder his wife was bereft at his passing!'

His name? Johnny Torrio.

What was Torrio's business? Over time, the Capone-Torrio mobsters raked in billions from bootlegging, prostitution, loan-sharking and gambling. However, his ten-hour working day in Chicago was chiefly concerned with 'the brothel business, allocating girls from house to house, cutting corners on the food and linen bills, calculating the previous night's profits,' said Cooke.

Torrio attributed no humanity to the girls he handled. He thought of them as 'commodities' to be bought, sold and replaced when worn out. His was the largest prostitution racket in America.

Yet Torrio was, externally, squeaky-clean. He never missed confession and mass. He had been raised as a good Catholic by his Italian mother and, throughout his years as *Capo Mafioso*, was always considered 'a religious man'.

An extreme example of the problem with religion. But a valid one?

Chapter 7

Good News

Those who attack religion often make the mistake of regarding Christianity as a 'religion'. It does not belong in that category. Unique among world faiths, Christianity is *not* a religion.

Joanie (chapter 5) was attracted to Christianity by one lifestyle indicator she noticed in her youth pastor. Later, that same youth pastor and his wife, together with Jay and others, led her to a deeper understanding of Christianity.

What enabled Joanie to experience new birth was when she was introduced to the bottom line of new-birth theology in Ephesians chapter 2 verses 8, 9 and 10. The Good News summarised in those verses is what disqualifies Christianity as a religion. More important than that, it introduced Joanie to the character and Person of Jesus – and, through Him, the character and Person of God. In essence, she grasped that *the* Good News is Good News about God.

Religion, we have noticed, involves belief in a man-made god and the effort to achieve some sort of 'salvation' by obedience to

Good News

rules and rituals associated with that god.

Christianity's bottom line is expressed in Paul's letter to the Ephesians (2:8, 9, 10):

'For it is by grace you have been saved, through faith – and this not from yourselves, it is the gift of God – not by works, so that no-one can boast. For we are God's workmanship, created in Christ Jesus to do good works . . .'

The Good News summarised in those verses is explained by the apostle Paul in the Letter to the Romans, chapters 3 to 8.

Paul – then known as Saul – had been Christianity's principal opponent in the years following its birth. His aim had been to use the shock troops of the Jewish establishment to strangle the new movement in its infancy. His efforts had extended beyond Judea to cities elsewhere with Jewish populations. By the time he led his shock troops to Damascus, his reputation among Christians was as the principal enemy of the faith. For them, Saul was some sort of monster.

That Christianity's destroyer became its principal champion owed something to what Saul had seen of Christians facing death for their faith. It owed more, however, to the Risen Christ's personal intervention in Saul's life as he approached Damascus, where he experienced 'conversion'.

Saul, renamed Paul, took time out for three or more years of study. His sources would have been the Old Testament Scriptures as they related to the coming Messiah-King, in which he found the coming of Jesus clearly foreshadowed. It also involved countless interviews with the personal witnesses to Christ's life, death and resurrection. Years later he would tell Christians in Corinth that some hundreds of such witnesses were still alive and available for interview (1 Corinthians 15:3-8).

By the time Paul began his extensive travels, he had a clear grasp of what the life, ministry, death and resurrection of Jesus meant. The meaning that he found was relevant to all people, not just Jews. Paul took advantage of the peace imposed upon the world by the Romans. He was helped by the common culture and language the Romans brought with them, and the excellent roads they had built. Paul became a travelling missionary, preaching to Gentiles as well as Jews.

So successful was the mission to the Gentiles that scholars believe that, by AD 60, for every one Jewish Christian there were 100,000 Gentile Christians.

Paul kept in touch by letter with the churches he had founded. The letters he sent to them were carried from congregation to congregation by church leaders. There they were read aloud. The letters addressed local problems. More important, they clearly and tirelessly explained and defended the Christian Good News.

Years later a source hostile to Christianity maintained that that Good News had 'turned the world upside down'. Another such source said that Christianity spread around the Mediterranean world like 'wildfire'.

The Good News was changing the world. The change was brought about by the message preached by the missionaries, together with the supernatural power of the Holy Spirit that both drove them *and* made minds receptive to its life-transforming gist.

That life-transforming gist – as expressed in the Letter to the Ephesians (2:8, 9, 10) and in many other letters – was rooted in the life and teaching of Jesus.

It is, therefore, important to come to grips with the four Gospels before we unpack the Good News as Paul wrote it down in his letters to the churches.

Chapter 8

Rooted in the Gospels

That Christianity was not a religion was evident in the teachings and actions of Jesus.

Jesus called people away from rules-and-rituals 'salvation', by personifying and preaching grace.

The taproot of grace is in the Story of the Lost Son.

Before we examine it, let's first look at what Jesus said about religion –and, second, examine and unpack His mission statement, in which He summarises His teaching on salvation.

Jesus: opposed to religion

Jesus Christ spoke out against religion. Indeed, I would argue that He is the most anti-religious Person of all. Of half a hundred things Jesus said to the religious people of His own day, this one sums up that anti-religious attitude: 'You travel over land and sea to win a single convert, and when he becomes one, you make him twice as much a son of hell as you are' (Matthew 23:15). Tough talking in anybody's language.

Part of the reason for Christ's depth of feeling against religion

Knowing Jesus *Knowing* God

was that He knew that hypocrisy was the common denominator among the rules-and-rituals men. He said, '. . . they do not practise what they preach. They tie up heavy loads and put them on men's shoulders, but they themselves are not willing to lift a finger to move them' (Matthew 23:3, 4). They burdened people with endless rules, and then stood back and watched them stagger through life beneath their weight.

Jesus did not come to impose burdens, but to help us carry the ones we already have. 'Come to me, all you who are weary and burdened,' He says, 'and I will give you rest. Take my yoke upon you and learn from me . . . and you will find rest for your souls. For my yoke is easy and my burden is light.' (Matthew 11:28-30.)

A fiver's worth of God plus endless rules and rituals was *what Jesus called people away from!*

Mission statement

When Jesus went on the record at the beginning of His ministry, His opener was a little like a mission statement: 'The time has come. . . . The kingdom of God is near. Repent and believe the good news!' (Mark 1:15.) He then proceeded to call people away from their comfort zones to a radical new way of life. And 'radical' *is* the right word.

To understand what Jesus said, we need to unpack three terms He used:

1. Repentance

2. The Kingdom of God

3. The Good News (aka 'the Gospel').

1. Repentance. Evangelical preachers in past decades have tended to narrow the meaning down to something like this: an emotional sense of guilt, identified and acted upon at one particular time.

Repentance means much more than that. The 'religious' have worked in guilt as some artists work in oils.

Rooted in the Gospels

Jesus said, 'Repent and believe the good news!' That sounds like two things. In fact, it is one thing. 'Leave London and go to Lincoln' sounds like two things. It is one thing in the sense that you cannot go to Lincoln without leaving London. Through repentance you have embraced the Good News. By embracing the Good News, you have entered the Kingdom of God. Our 1, 2 and 3 are, therefore, three in one. Like the Trinity!

Repentance is so much more than sin-sorrow, though it may begin there.

Repentance is much more than turning your back on something bad, though that is a part of it.

These two definitions may help us:

'Repentance is that mighty change of mind, heart and life brought about by the Spirit of God.'

'Repentance is a change of mind about sin, self and the Saviour.'

Repentance is a reorientation of one's whole life. The best metaphor for it is a 180-degree turn.

What was ahead of you, pre-repentance, is behind you, post-repentance. There is an about face. Good and evil change places. You walk in the opposite direction – in the company of the living Christ.

2. The Kingdom of God. Where you walk is into the Kingdom of God. This Kingdom is a Kingdom of Grace throughout, but ends in the Kingdom of Glory.

Life priorities are reordered in God's Kingdom. That is what makes it so radical. After His mission statement Jesus began calling people away from their jobs and families. 'But vocation and family are what define us,' we protest. And that is true. However, even they cannot take priority over the Kingdom of God.

Here is a case in point.

Dr and Mrs McCoy had raised their sons on Kingdom priorities.

Knowing *Jesus* Knowing *God*

Among these was to rest and worship on the seventh day of the week, which, according to Scripture, 'is the Sabbath of the Lord your God'. When the boys were, respectively, 16 and 18, they were under a great deal of pressure to succeed in state examinations. Success in those examinations was necessary for entry into medical school in order for them to follow their father's profession. On the weekend immediately prior to their exams, Dr McCoy encouraged his sons not only to stay home from church but to set aside the whole day for study.

Having been raised in the Sabbath-observing tradition, the sons believed that the subliminal message they had heard was this: 'We have always stressed that the Kingdom of God takes first priority – but, when push comes to shove, success in your career is Number One.'

The boys went to university, though not to read Medicine, and used their degrees as a platform for successful careers in the City.[1] While continuing with some of the ethical precepts they had been taught in childhood, they abandoned their beliefs and any connection with Christianity. Kingdom priorities were abandoned. Dr McCoy's most oft-repeated verse these days is Matthew's Gospel, chapter 6, verse 33, where Jesus says, 'But seek first [God's] kingdom and his righteousness, and all these things will be given to you as well.'

Not long after Jesus issued His mission statement (Mark 1:15) and called His disciples away from their secular priorities to Kingdom priorities, He led them in worship at the synagogue. Following that, He went with Peter to his home and healed a member of his family. Clearly, family is a Kingdom priority, too.

Jesus' call was for people to accompany Him on a journey into His Kingdom. In those days followers usually chose rabbis. Jesus, by contrast, chose His followers. On the journey on which He led them, there was no turning back.

When followers of Jesus choose to turn away from the

Rooted in the Gospels

Kingdom, the Kingdom does not crush them. Jesus was crushed so that His followers might enter it.

3. The Good News. 490 years before Christ, the Athenian army defeated the Persians at Marathon, thus driving them out of Greek territory. Victory in battle rarely has the positive effect that has been attributed to this one. It has been argued that the victory at Marathon made possible the 500 years in which Greek culture – language, literature, philosophy, architecture, mathematics, politics, sculpture – blossomed and became universal. On the basis of this, John Stuart Mill called Marathon 'the most important battle in history'.

From the battlefield, heralds ran the 26 miles back to the city of Athens with this message:

'We have fought for you and we have won. Now you are no longer slaves. You are free.'

The Greek word for this message was *euangelion*. The prefix *eu* means 'joyful'. The remainder of the word comes from *angelos*, which means 'news'. This Greek word – often used in a secular context – is the one translated *Good News* in the New Testament.

Behind the Christian Good News is victory in a battle far greater than that of Marathon, though the Good News taken to the world by Christianity's heralds is not too dissimilar to that conveyed by those who ran the 26 miles from Marathon to Athens.

The consequence to those who believe Christianity's Good News is, in the words of J. I. Packer,[2] 'the truly dramatic transition from the status of a condemned criminal awaiting a terrible sentence to that of an heir awaiting a fabulous inheritance'.

---

[1] The commercial heart of London.
[2] *Knowing God*, J. I. Packer, Hodder and Stoughton: UK, 1973.

Knowing *Jesus* Knowing **God**

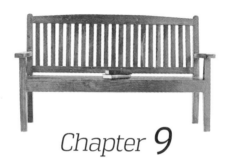

Chapter 9

The Case of the Lost Son

Jesus was a brilliant Communicator. He had come into the world to show us God. This He did by some challenging teaching and by living up to all of it. He asked His enemies, 'Which of you can truthfully accuse me of sin?' (John 8:46, NLT) and neither expected – nor received – a single reply!

But Jesus communicated His most memorable lessons through stories or parables. The parable that tells us most about God is the Story of the Lost Son, misleadingly referred to as 'the Prodigal Son'. Why misleading?

The English word *prodigal* means 'generous to the point of wastefulness'. The 'son' in the story is wasteful, but not generous. The Father, by contrast, is 'generous to the point of wastefulness' – from start to finish. So if the word *prodigal* is used in the story's title it had better be 'The Story of the Prodigal Father'. And the story *was* told to showcase the Father. However, if, as we tend to, we give the son the starring role, then the title had better refer to the *lost* son. Of course, giving the starring role to the younger of

The Case of the Lost Son

the Father's two sons is made entirely appropriate in that each of us gives himself the starring role in his own life story.

That's not a bad start, since Jesus meant the story to be about us and our salvation, as well as about the Person of God. However, He gives us a choice as to which of the two sons we will choose to identify with.

The chapter which contains, in order, the stories of the Lost Sheep, the Lost Coin and the Lost Son (Luke 15) begins with this narrative:

'Tax collectors and other notorious sinners often came to listen to Jesus teach. This made the Pharisees and teachers of religious law complain that he was associating with such sinful people – even eating with them!' (Verses 1 and 2, NLT.)

Jesus was, by His three stories, addressing the issue raised by the religious people ('Pharisees and teachers of religious law') and giving hope to those they considered lost and unfit for purpose. The gist was that there was more hope for the 'lost' than for the 'religious'. Elsewhere He said to the religious: 'I tell you the truth, corrupt tax collectors and prostitutes will get into the Kingdom of God before you do.' (Matthew 21:31, NLT.) To Jesus, apparently, religion was a problem, not a pathway to God. Those who stood a chance of being accepted by God were those who acknowledged, first, their status as sinners (or 'lost').

Three stories, then, each with something or someone who was lost.

Story one: **the lost sheep.** The Shepherd goes out in search, and finds the lost. There is rejoicing when it is brought back to the fold. (Luke 15:3-6.)

Story two: **the lost coin.** The poor woman who has lost the coin searches for it, and finds it. When it is found there is rejoicing. (Luke 15:8, 9.)

Knowing *Jesus* Knowing **God**

The pattern: **A loss. A search. Rejoicing and celebration.**

By way of explanation for the rejoicing, Jesus says (vs. 10, NLT): 'In the same way, there is joy in the presence of God's angels when even one sinner repents.' That tells us what the stories are about, and, at the same time, prepares us for the third. But watch out! An element present in the first two stories is absent from the third. Jesus expects us to spot that.

Story three: **the lost son.**

'A man had two sons. The younger son told his father, "I want my share of your estate now before you die." So his father agreed to divide his wealth between his sons.' 15:11, 12, NLT.

The lad was heartless. He wanted his share of the family fortune, and he was not prepared to wait around for it until his father died.

The father had no legal obligation to do anything for his younger son, but he did. Almost certainly he would have had to sell off land. When the lad was united with his fortune, he showed his father a clean pair of heels and went to 'a distant land, and there he wasted all his money in wild living' (vs. 13, NLT).

Familiar, so far. But the 'wild living' stuff was not up to expectations, and in any event the money ran out. That situation was bad enough, but it coincided with a meltdown in the distant land's economy, with resultant shortages. Hunger drove the lost lad to seek employment on a pig farm. He thought that was the ultimate humiliation, until he realised he still could not afford basic rations and found himself looking hungrily at the food he was feeding to the pigs.

The lost son 'came to his senses' and realised that even the hired hands on his father's farm had enough food and to spare. He rehearsed a speech he would make to his father in which he would offer his services as a hired hand, and set off on the long road home.

The Case of the Lost Son

The lad was expecting the frosty reception that he deserved. The Father, however, was prodigal to a fault. Remember: *generous to the point of wastefulness*. Seeing his son returning, the Father ran to meet him, 'while he was still a long way off' (vs. 20). 'Filled with love and compassion, [the Father] ran to his son, embraced him, and kissed him. His son said to him, "Father, I have sinned against both heaven and you, and I am no longer worthy of being called your son . . ." ' (vss. 20, 21, NLT). His next words were to be, 'so please take me on as a hired servant,' but the Father interrupted. The lad was not given a chance to finish.

The Prodigal Father embraced him. He ordered that the son be given 'the finest robe': affirming that he was being received as an heir, and a cherished one at that. To reinforce the same message and to give him authority, a special ring was placed on the lad's finger. To remove any possible doubt that the basis on which the lost boy had been received on his return was as a son, sandals were put on his feet.

The 'lost sheep' and 'lost coin' stories had ended with a joyful celebration. The lost son was received with a party thrown in his honour.

Prodigal. Generous to the point of wastefulness.

The Prodigal Father, then; not the prodigal younger son. And not the prodigal older son, either. There was nothing prodigal about him!

'Meanwhile, the older son was in the fields working. . . .' (Vs. 25.) Hearing the loud music of celebration coming from the house, he returned to the farmhouse and asked a servant what was going on. 'Your brother is back,' he was told. . . . 'We are celebrating because of his safe return' (vs. 27, NLT). The older brother was incandescent.

The Father pleads with the older brother. The reinstatement of the returning wastrel was at *his* expense. No celebration had ever been held in *his* honour. He would have no part in the celebration,

Knowing Jesus Knowing God

no matter how long his father pleaded. He was angry that his Father could forgive such a sinner. After all, he, the faithful brother, had worked hard for what he had achieved.

Jesus ended the story like this:

'His father said to him, "Look, dear son, you have always stayed by me, and everything I have is yours. We had to celebrate this happy day. For your brother was dead and has come back to life! He was lost, but now he is found!" ' (Vss. 31, 32, NLT.)

The story ends with the Father holding the door open, but the elder brother stubbornly standing outside the party. The younger brother is a returning sinner. The Father models God's grace. The elder brother was religious. And he was outside, and refusing to enter.

Who was 'generous to the point of wastefulness'? That's how it is with the Father's grace. The religious are instinctively opposed to it. They have *worked* for what they have, and anyone who has not is unacceptable to them. They are not, however, unacceptable to the Father. When the lost come home, it is as if the dead have come alive. And if that's not worth a celebration. . . .

Jesus' audience would have no trouble identifying the cast of characters. Only those with a longer attention span would pick up on the need for a fourth character.

In the Lost Sheep and Lost Coin stories the pattern of '1. Loss; 2. Search; 3. Celebration' had been established.

In the Lost Son story only the Loss and Celebration elements had been present. Who had gone to the distant country in search of the lost son?

No one.

Who could have?

An authentic older brother.

The story as Jesus told it leaves us longing for a true older brother. One who would leave home and go in search of his

The Case of the Lost Son

younger sibling in the distant land.

When lost sons and daughters return to the Father's house, the Father runs to meet them and smothers them in His warm embrace. That's grace.

The bitter, ungracious older brother makes us long for a true older brother who, carrying out the Father's strategy, goes in search of lost siblings.

A true older brother shares the prodigality of the Father. As the Good Shepherd goes in search of lost sheep, the *true* older brother seeks for lost siblings in the streets and sin joints of the distant land.

The true older brother is prepared to pay a high price to forgive, redeem and restore lost brothers and sisters.

When we see the Father's perfect Son with arms outstretched and nailed to a crossbeam, we see Him paying the price of redemption.

The Good Shepherd gives His life for the sheep (John 10:14-18).

There is a sense in which the Father's embrace is made possible by the sacrifice of the *true* Older Brother, Jesus Himself.

The central Character of the Bible's Revelation Play is the Author.

The central Character – the *true* Older Brother – in the Lost Son story, which summarises the message of the Bible, is the Narrator.

Chapter *10*

Jesus: Lord of the Sabbath – and End of Religion

Having spent a lot of my working life around religious people, I can totally understand why Jesus preferred the company of publicans and sinners.

It was not just a preference for their company, however. Their priority was reflected in both His mission and His message. He said that He had not come to call the righteous, but the sinners. The opening sentence of His Manifesto of the Kingdom (also known as the Sermon on the Mount) promised 'the Kingdom of Heaven' to 'the poor in spirit'.

'Why? What had they done?' we might ask. The answer, of course, is 'Nothing'. They had done nothing, and they knew it. By definition 'the poor in spirit' knew that the only way they could receive salvation was if God gave it to them.

Jesus fell foul of the Pharisees, the religious people, very early on in His ministry. They could just about live with the idea of a travelling healer, but as soon as Jesus emerged as the Saviour they began to plot His murder. Jesus first emerged as Saviour in a

Jesus: Lord of the Sabbath – and End of Religion

seaside town in which He had a lot of popular support.

Jesus was preaching in a house. The fact that He never did so again was probably down to the consequences for the house-owner.

Soon the whole of the house, and the area immediately surrounding it, was jam-packed with people. Four men who arrived late, carrying a paralysed friend on a stretcher, could not get through the jumble of humanity to bring him to the attention of Jesus. Certain Jesus could help their friend, they became astonishingly resourceful. Somehow they got him onto the roof, and, immediately above where Jesus was speaking, they began to dig their way through the roof. Roofs were made of something between mud and thatch then, so *dig* is the right word.

Imagine the multitude – both the ordinary and the religious – as they began to see daylight above them. Imagine the feelings of the house-owner. . . . If he was hoping for just a little hole through which someone could shout, 'Hey! Jesus! You're needed up here!' he was in for disappointment. They dug a hole to the dimensions of their paralysed friend – perhaps five-and-a-half feet long and two-and-a-half feet across – and proceeded to lower their friend down at the feet of Jesus.

When they had done this successfully, they left the rest to Jesus. If they were expecting 'Be healed and walk!' they were shocked. Jesus said, 'Son, your sins are forgiven' (Mark 2:5, NKJV).

After a searching look at the paralysed man, Jesus must have decided that suffering was not his number one problem. It was as if He had said to the man, 'You've come here for physical healing, but the greater need is for spiritual healing. Don't underestimate the depths of your need. We'll tackle spiritual and physical healing together!'

That put the cat well and truly among the pigeons as far as the religious contingent were concerned. Though they resented the popular following of Jesus the Healer, they could live with it, just about. Jesus as Saviour, however, was way outside the comfort zone of their ideas. When Jesus forgave the man's sins He took a long and very deliberate stride down the road to Calvary. Jesus as Saviour was Jesus as God. That they could not handle.

It became clear to the religious people that Jesus had *not* come to reform religion, a cause with which they would have had some sympathy. He had come to *end* religion. Indeed, *He had come to replace religion with Himself*. His enemies sensed that, and felt threatened. They asked, 'What next?'

Next Jesus challenged them on the Law and went to its heart to do so: the Sabbath.

The Pharisees had done an EU (European Union) job on the Sabbath commandment. God had prescribed rest, not work, on the Sabbath. The Pharisees had taken 'work' and divided it up into more categories than you could count, and had placed them under thirty-nine subheadings. One Sabbath, as they walked through the fields, the disciples of Jesus were picking ears of corn and eating the grain. That seriously overheated the collars of the onlooking Pharisees. The disciples were infringing no fewer than four of the thirty-nine categories of work prohibition: reaping, threshing, winnowing and preparing food.

Not only did Jesus fail to adopt the judgemental mood of the religious people towards His disciples, but He went on into the synagogue and healed a man with a withered hand whom he found there. That broke at least one more category of the Pharisees' prohibitions on work. Probably more.

Jesus said, 'The Sabbath was made for man. Man wasn't made for the Sabbath' (Mark 2:27, paraphrased).

Jesus did not defend working on God's day. He did, however, suggest that more important principles were at stake than their homemade EU-style prohibitions. There was more to the Sabbath than earning brownie points with God by observing obscure rules.

Jesus: Lord of the Sabbath – and End of Religion

Indeed, that was not the point at all. 'The Sabbath was made for man' and Jesus, as 'Lord of the Sabbath', wanted to restore its true significance (Mark 2:27, 28, NKJV).

In the cornfield Jesus did not deny that His disciples had been careless about traditional observances. Instead He pleaded special circumstances (human need) and a biblical precedent. The precedent was when David, because of his hunger and the hunger of his men, had appropriated the consecrated bread in 'the house of God' (Mark 2:25, 26). David had done that in the period between his anointing by Samuel and when he was actually enthroned. Jesus was the Anointed One (*Christ* means 'Anointed One'), but He would not be enthroned until He had Golgotha and the empty tomb behind Him. Nevertheless, as the Anointed One, He was already Lord of the Sabbath and He was replacing rules and rituals by the Kingdom of God. Kingdom considerations replaced neither the Law nor its heart, the Sabbath. They did, however, provide a whole new set of attitudes and priorities which were closer to God's original intentions regarding the Sabbath. The Sabbath was made for man's benefit: as a 'delight' and as a sign that those who celebrated it already belonged to God.

Make my day

In the synagogue, the religious people appeared at a particular disadvantage. 'Some of them were looking for a reason to accuse Jesus, so they watched him closely to see if he would heal [the man with the shrivelled hand] on the Sabbath.' (Mark 3:2.) It was as if they were saying, 'Make my day – and we'll have you!'

Jesus exposed the bankruptcy of their religious world view by asking them, ' "Which is lawful on the Sabbath: to do good or to do evil, to save life or to kill?" But they remained silent' (vs. 4). Their only response when Jesus healed the man was to initiate a conspiracy to murder Jesus (vs. 6). How's that for religion?

Knowing *Jesus* Knowing *God*

Where religion is, politics is never far away. Students of history find it difficult not to spare some sympathy for Richard Dawkins' contention that religion's influence on history has been largely malignant.

Simon Sebag Montefiore's *Jerusalem: The Biography* is a history of that city from the earliest times to its liberation at the end of the Six-Day War of 1967. Reading the narrative it is hard to avoid the conclusion that, from the first, there has not been a square foot of land in and around Jerusalem that has not been drenched in blood. Further, that much of the blood-letting has been done in the name of religion, and that the worst atrocities were committed by the crusader kings with their toxic mix of politics, religion and primitive bloodlust.

That toxic mix, and the behaviour to which it gave rise, is indefensible. It had no connection whatever with Jesus and the New Testament Gospel.

At the core of religion are rules, rituals and the means of their aggressive imposition on others.

At the heart of the Gospel is grace.

Religion and Christianity are two completely different things. Jesus did not come to reform religion, but to replace it. He came to replace it with Himself and His Gospel. Nowhere is this clearer than in His Sabbath teaching.

Immediately before Jesus healed the man on the Sabbath, the record says, 'He looked round at them in anger and [was] deeply distressed at their stubborn hearts' (vs. 5).

What made Jesus angry?

Their religion.

The religious people did not want Jesus to heal the man because it would have infringed their rules.

The problem with them was their religion, and the fact that it had caused them to pervert the whole meaning of the Sabbath.

Jesus: Lord of the Sabbath – and End of Religion

And that was?

- Rest for the weary and the stressed.
- The recharging of spiritual batteries.
- Repairing that which is broken in our lives, and replenishing what is drained.

Jesus was angry with the religious people because the nature of their religion – especially with regard to the Sabbath – had made them guilty of spiritual oppression.

Religious people had turned the Sabbath God meant as 'a delight' (Isaiah 58:13, 14) into a means of spiritual abuse.

Religion says: I obey – therefore I am accepted.

The Gospel says: I'm fully accepted in Jesus – therefore I obey joyfully.

Jesus taught that the Sabbath of which He is Lord is 'made for man' and that its original principle is rest.

The word Sabbath *(Shabbat)* means *deep rest*, *deep peace*. It is a near synonym of the word *shalom*. English, usually a rich language, has real difficulty translating the Hebrew word *shalom*. The best it can do is peace; but *shalom* means so much more than that. It is a word from God's vocabulary, and means 'a state in which you are truly whole, and flourishing in every department of life'. Hence the Sabbath greeting 'Shabbat shalom' means, 'May the Sabbath replenish and restore you in every area of your life.' That is what God wants to do for you through His Sabbath. '[Then] you will find your joy in the LORD' (Isaiah 58:14).

Rest

Yes, the Sabbath is a very big deal.

But the physical and mental time-out of the once-a-week Sabbath is symbolic of another, deeper level of rest.

Religion imposes on people the never-ending work of self-justification.

God wants us to experience true rest through the Gospel.

Knowing Jesus *Knowing* **God**

You accept that rest when you accept that Jesus lived the life you should have lived and died the death you should have died.

Jesus experienced restlessness on the cross when He said, 'My God, My God – WHY?' It was the result of His experience of total separation from His Father because He carried the collective weight of human sin. He went through that so that we need never experience that restlessness, the separation.

When Jesus told the paralysed man, 'Your sins are forgiven', He was claiming to be God. Central to the teaching of Jesus is that identity claim. The basis of the claim is that Life became flesh and blood in the Person of Jesus, and walked the streets of our planet.

Because Jesus made that claim, and did so repeatedly, we cannot patronise Him, as some have tried to do, by saying, 'Oh, He was just a very great teacher.' C. S. Lewis rightly said that Jesus was either mad, or bad, or God. No one is saying He is mad or bad. How could they? If Jesus is who He says He is – *and He is!* – then I must fall at His feet and call Him God and Saviour.

The Good News (the Gospel) made possible by the death and resurrection of Jesus does not say, 'The good are in and the bad are out.' Jesus came to save sinners: those who know that they are morally or spiritually unable to save themselves. The Kingdom of Heaven, you will recall, is for 'the poor in spirit'.

On the cross the Lord of the Sabbath said, 'It is finished.' If we accept that He did that on our behalf, we can rest from religion – for ever.

Jesus is the end of religion.

In place of religion we have Jesus and His liberating Good News.

'There remains, then, a Sabbath-rest for the people of God' (Hebrews 4:9). It is a rest from religion.

Chapter 11

One Solitary Figure

I didn't know *who* I was angry with – society? God? The BBC? – I just knew I was very, very angry. Too angry, in fact, to sleep.

If I am playing with the remote after the 9pm watershed and come across something that upsets me in a TV drama, I just turn it off. However, if it's a documentary, I'm apt to convince myself that it's something I should know about.

That late-night documentary, occasioned by the Madeleine McCann disappearance, had included footage about a global slave trade in children. The soundtrack had featured the assertion that, for every publicised abduction, there were thousands every year that received little or no publicity. That was what put sleep out of bounds. I recalled the thrice-repeated assertion by Jesus that the child-abuser would have been better experiencing deep-sea drowning with a millstone about his neck.

When photo-journalists cover mega-bad news stories of 'atrocities', or events inadequately described as 'natural disasters' – bombings, floods, tsunamis – they contrive to have a single, solitary figure in the foreground of the picture. The drooping figure, stage right, silhouetted against the foreground of the hurricane-blasted shoreline or the bombed landscape, serves to add poignancy.

In my years as a teacher I used a film about the liberation of the concentration camps. At one point corpses were moved, a few at a time, by a JCB-type machine, while a single, solitary survivor looked on. Girls watching often wept, while boys betrayed an untamed anger.

Statistics sanitise horrors of scale. But when we see the solitary, grieving figure in the foreground, it brings the horror home. It is then that we react emotionally and ask, 'Where is God? Doesn't He care?'

John wrote his Gospel to introduce the Greek world to the mind of God revealed in Jesus. The main presupposition of the Greeks with regard to gods was summed up in the word *apatheia* (apathy): the gods couldn't care less.

Hence everything about the God revealed in Jesus caught the Greeks napping. Nowhere would they have been more shocked than in John's eleventh chapter.

Lazarus of Bethany died. Four days later Jesus arrived. Martha, sister of Lazarus, rebuked Him and, by implication, held Him responsible for Lazarus's death. Having done that, she demanded that He *do* something! 'Your brother will rise again,' Jesus told her.

' "Yes," Martha said, "he will rise when everyone else rises, at the last day." ' (John 11:24, NLT.) She seems to have said that truculently, as if to imply, 'But that doesn't help *here, now*. . . .'

What Jesus said next shook Jews and close friends as much as it shook Greeks: ' "I am the resurrection and the life. He who believes in me will live, even though he dies; and whoever lives and believes in me will never die." ' (Verses 25, 26.)

One Solitary Figure

Jesus was saying that those who identified with Him received eternal life; physical death was not their ultimate end. John's Gospel had begun with the words, 'In the beginning was the Word. . . . In him was life . . .' (John 1:1-4). It would conclude with the thought that its whole point had been 'that you may believe . . . and that by believing you may have life . . .' (20:31).

Jesus' reply to Martha was the fullest expression of His claim to be the Source of the indestructible life of the resurrection. He was the actual life of the deathless God Himself. The resurrection that triumphs over death was not confined to the distant future. It was here in the present, embodied in the One who is the Resurrection and the Life. To believe in Jesus means to believe that death has been defeated.

Jesus' words when uttered – and when read subsequently in John's account – would have been received as a bombshell declaration.

Shortly afterwards, when Lazarus's other sister Mary arrived, she laid the same guilt trip on Jesus that Martha had, before she broke into sobs.

The part of the story that collided most violently with John's readers' expectations of God was what came next (11:33-38). It begins (NLT), 'When Jesus saw her weeping . . . deep anger welled up within him, and he was deeply troubled.' John's description of Jesus' reaction (which he uses again in verse 38) is *embrimaomai*. Translated from the Greek, it is a word for a deep human emotion we would not normally associate with Jesus: *rage*, *outrage*.

John wants us to know that, as Jesus approached the grave of Lazarus, He was not in a state of uncontrollable grief, but of inexpressible anger, even outrage. Indeed, He was so outraged that He wept.

How's that for an insight into the mind of God?

Why would Jesus be so angry – when He knew He was about

to restore Lazarus to life?

Some have suggested that the outrage resulted from the shallow, pretended grief of the 'professional mourners' who accompanied Mary and Martha. Surely not! Jesus was a Jew and accustomed to this phenomenon. At least it showed solidarity in the face of the last enemy.

Others suggest that Jesus was outraged at Mary and Martha's lack of faith. Surely not! Both women had expressed absolute faith in Him (verses 27 and 32). Martha had said, 'I believe that you are the Christ, the Son of God. . . .'

So why was Jesus angry? Why did He weep? One translator suggests that He was so angry 'his body trembled'!

The spectacle of the grief of Mary, Martha and their friends reminded Jesus of the age-old tyranny of evil, of all that went with it, and of evil's first cause.

Approaching the tomb of Lazarus, Jesus was, above all, enraged at the tyranny of death. In the grief of Mary He sees and feels the misery of the whole race. He burns with rage at the oppressor of humankind. Death was the object of his wrath – and, behind death, death's demented instigator.

As Jesus approached the tomb of Lazarus, He did so like a Champion preparing for battle. He had come to terminate the reign of the terminator.

The one solitary figure, grieving in the foreground of every disaster, injustice and scene of suffering; the unidentified mourner at billions of funerals – had stopped stooping – pulled Himself up to His full height, and on His face was the pent-up rage of centuries. One day the world will see that rage again (Revelation 6:16).

Outside Bethany a Voice echoed that even the dead could hear.

We ask, 'Does God care?' It is a feeble question. God is the omniscient One. He knows, He cares, He feels. . . . A student

One Solitary Figure

missionary sees a leprosy sufferer and is genuinely sympathetic. Then he goes to his room and thinks about something else. He cannot suffer the physical sensations; AND the loss of dignity, the ostracism and the loneliness of the leprosy sufferer. God can and does. It is an aspect of His great grace.

The outrage that we experience at the evils and injustices of the world are not even a pale reflection of the outrage God feels.

'Our world is a vast lazar house, a scene of misery that we dare not allow even our thoughts to dwell upon. Did we realise it as it is, the burden would be too terrible. *Yet God feels it all.*' Ellen G. White, *Education*, p. 264.

When the solitary grieving Man who mourns our tragedies stands to His full height there will be both tears and outrage on His face. That Voice that cried, 'Lazarus, come out!' will sound again. 'For the Lord Himself will come down from heaven with a commanding shout' (1 Thessalonians 4:16, NLT). At that shout the myriads of Heaven will be summoned to Earth. And, on Earth, the dead in Christ will hear again the Voice of the One who is the Resurrection and the Life – and they will rise.

But not just THEN – RIGHT NOW Christ *is* the Resurrection and the Life.

When the Lord brings salvation to a person He cancels the curse of sin, frees the captives, reverses the effect of death and secures that person forever in His heavenly Kingdom.

Death no more shall have dominion. . . . In a moment the dead shall be raised incorruptible. . . . This mortal shall put on immortality. Then shall be brought to pass the saying that is written, 'Death shall be swallowed up in victory.'

Chapter 12

How the Old Order Ended

Lazarus, dead for four days, heard the voice of Jesus, rose to life, was freed from his grave clothes, carried on his life in Bethany, and was present at a major community event in his honour. The embarrassment of the authorities that Lazarus, known to have died, was now very much alive, was such that it accelerated the plan to murder or otherwise dispose of Jesus. There was a plot to murder Lazarus, too, but that did not come off. (John 11:43-50; 12:1-11.)

The use of Jesus' supernatural power against death and disease shows God's attitude towards those unwelcome phenomena. The rage of Jesus against death and disease (John 11:33, 38) is God's rage, too.

In face of all the wretchedness of humanity, God says, ' "Oh, that . . . my eyes [were] a fountain of tears" ' (Jeremiah 9:1). The outpouring of God's anger and the torrent of grief that Niagaras from His eyes will one day, according to the Bible, wash away all of it – every trace of the old order.

How the Old Order Ended

When we see the single, solitary onlooker viewing the scenes of destruction and devastation we identify with Him and, in a small way, experience His rage. We ask, 'Does God care?' and, in face of the evidence, it is a feeble question.

God is the *omniscient* One. He not only knows all. He feels, experiences, all.

He knows. He cares. He feels.

The pain is His pain.

The rage is His rage.

The old order cannot last.

We cannot share the loss of dignity, loneliness and ostracism of the leprosy sufferer. God can. God does. It is an aspect of His character and His grace.

The outrage we feel at the evils and injustices of the world is not even a pale reflection of the outrage God feels. But we feel it because God hardwired it into us. He made us. The rage *we* feel is a small part of the proof that *He* made us.

God is not just our Creator. He is truly *Immanuel* – God *with* us – even in our worst sufferings.

God is tri-personal. That is the message with which John's Gospel begins. Jesus was not created. He took part in creation. He has lived through all eternity in the intimacy of the Father. 'No-one has ever seen God, but God the One and Only [Son], who is at the Father's side, has made him known.' (John 1:18.)

But what would happen should the Father and Son separate? What could separate them?

All four Gospel narratives indicate that Jesus did not face up to His impending death with the fearless heroism shown by great martyrs both before and after His time.

The Maccabean martyrs who, in the centuries before Christ's birth, died under the tyranny of Antiochus Epiphanes, did so defiantly, speaking confidently of God.

Thousands of martyrs in the centuries after Christ, though in agony, made defiant declarations. The two men who were burned to death where the Martyr's Monument stands in Oxford were Hugh Latimer and Nicholas Ridley. Even as he burned, Latimer said to his friend, 'Be of good cheer, Master Ridley, and play the man! We shall this day light such a candle by God's grace in England as I trust shall never be put out!' Nor has it been.

Jesus, by contrast, in Gethsemane before His agonies began, cried, 'My soul is overwhelmed with sorrow to the point of death. . . .' Peter, James and John reported that He was 'deeply distressed and troubled' (another use of *embrimaomai*). Mark 14:33, 34, TNIV. Matthew, Mark and Luke report that Jesus asked His Father to find another way through, before concluding, 'Yet not what I will, but what you will.'

From the cross Jesus cried, 'My God, my God, why have you forsaken me?' (Matthew 27:46.)

Why was Jesus far more overwhelmed by His death than the martyrs were?

At one level it was a cry of affirmation – '*My* God!' Don't miss the language of intimacy. It is the key to everything.

The death of Jesus was not the death of a martyr; and was qualitatively different from every other death. At the heart of that difference was *not* the hideous sufferings that came with crucifixion, made much of by filmmakers.

The worst agonies any of us face result from the loss of relationships we desperately want. When a colleague of some standing turns on you, berates you and subsequently separates himself from you – it hurts! If a girlfriend turns on you, says unforgettable things about you and walks away forever – it hurts even more! When a spouse does that, it hurts so that you wonder if you can ever recover!

But if a parent does it, the psychological damage to the child can be incalculable.

In Gethsemane, Jesus did not just lose filial or spousal love. On

How the Old Order Ended

the cross, He was missing more than the parental love He had had for a few years. He was bereft of the intimate love of the Father He had experienced from eternity past.

Christianity acknowledges that Jesus bore, as our Substitute, the weight of all our sin. Dying in our place, Jesus experienced the total exclusion from God that the human race has merited. He lived the life we should have lived and died the death we should have died.

In Gethsemane a measureless gulf between the eternal Son and the eternal Father yawned wider than eternity.

Jesus was not a martyr for some great cause. Uniquely, He died as our Substitute to pay the price of our sin, as only *He* could. His final cry on the cross was the ultimate cry of dereliction.

God became uniquely human in Jesus. Human enough to experience the worst of everything: poverty, rejection, despair, torture . . . but not until Gethsemane and Golgotha did He experience cosmic abandonment. The weight of the world's sin caused it. He bore that ultimate separation so that we should never have to do so. Because He bore it, the old order cannot last. Pain and evil will be removed. Death will die.

The Voice that called Lazarus from death will one day call every friend of Christ to life. (1 Thessalonians 4:13-17.) But at the end of Good Friday that Voice was silent and the body from which it came was dead and buried.

Chapter **13**

Who Is the Greatest?

On His way to Jerusalem for that final visit, and before He heard the heart-sinking news of Lazarus's death, Jesus and His disciples went through Jericho.

Two encounters they had in that ancient city communicate much about what Luke's Gospel adds to the picture of Jesus, and, therefore, the picture of God.

Mark (based, you will recall, on Peter's first-hand account) says that the disciples were talking politics as the party approached Jericho (Mark 10:32-52). For the third time, Jesus had told them that He was going to die in Jerusalem, but what preoccupied the disciples was which of them deserved the top jobs when Jesus established His Kingdom. Talk about gross insensitivity! Jesus used the two encounters in Jericho to teach them the only principles *He* needed them to know about politics. Luke's narrative is in his 18th chapter, verse 31, to his 19th chapter, verse 10.

The disciples were affronted by first the sound, then the sight of

Who Is the Greatest?

Bartimaeus the blind beggar. They had been absorbed among themselves with the question, 'Who is the greatest?' Jesus gave His attention to a noisy beggar whose name meant, in his native language, 'Son of Rubbish'. Bartimaeus represents the underclasses of the world: the Dalits (or Untouchables) on every continent. And India's Hindu-reinforced caste system is an outlandish caricature of the class system evident in most other countries. India's cities feature twenty-first-century skyscrapers below which the streets feature beggars and the legions of women with pots and pans balanced on their heads who might have thronged the streets twenty centuries ago, and every century since.

There have always been 'untouchables' and 'exploiters' – and before Jesus left Jericho for Jerusalem He had ministered to one from each 'class'.

As Jesus approached Jericho the word ran through the streets: 'Jesus is coming.' He was of interest to the population for a number of different reasons. Jericho was only 15 miles from Jerusalem, and was used as a dormitory town by the priesthood. Every member of the priestly class would be required to be at the Jerusalem Temple for the Passover. But that was still a week away when Jesus passed through, and most were still in town. They would have been part of the chorus of disapproval when blind Bartimaeus yelled, 'Jesus, Son of David, have mercy on me!' in a desperate attempt to attract the attention of Jesus.

But Bartimaeus would not 'Quiet down!' and, if anything, turned up the volume. He knew that Jesus was a Healer who paid attention to the marginalised and dispossessed. He was not about to miss his big chance. It was the chance of a lifetime.

That's all it took. Jesus called to him and he followed the sound of His voice. Soon the persistent, blind beggar was making even more noise praising God. He joined the Jesus party for the up-mountain trek from close, clammy Jericho to

Knowing *Jesus* Knowing **God**

cool, clear Jerusalem. At least he could see where he was going!

James and John – who had been particularly keen to be 'the greatest' – read the irony. Who would not?

Before the Jesus party left Jericho behind for the wheezing, wearisome trek up-mountain, there was another kind of 'untouchable' to be encountered, and another barrier to be surmounted.

If Bartimaeus was one of the poorest men in town, Zacchaeus was one of the richest. His untouchability lay in the way he had acquired his riches. He was a collaborator in the pay of the occupying Romans, and the best-hated man for miles. Zacchaeus was not making a noise to attract attention when we encounter him. He was sitting ever so quietly up a tree, hoping to catch his glimpse of Jesus without the attendant crowds catching sight of him. As long as nobody looked up. . . .

Jericho, situated where the Jordan flowed into the Dead Sea, commanded not just the Jordan Valley Road and the Jerusalem Road. It also commanded the principal river crossing to all points east. Consequently, it was the most lucrative taxation centre in Judea. Its chief tax collector was the best-hated, vertically-challenged Zacchaeus. The only way that notorious rascal could see Jesus and not be stabbed to death by a Zealot, or roughed up by the crowd, was to shin up a sycamore and sit quietly. What Zacchaeus didn't know was that not only did he want to see Jesus, but Jesus wanted to see *him!*

I have always suspected that the sight of a vertically-challenged, middle-aged, ample-waisted taxman perched up a tree must have been comical. Did Jesus smile when He saw him? To the multitude who followed the upward glance of Jesus, he might have become a jestingstock or worse – had not Jesus spoken first.

'Zacchaeus, come down immediately. I must stay at your house today.' (Luke 19:5, TNIV.)

Who Is the Greatest?

Imagine Zacchaeus's feelings when everyone looked up. Then imagine what the crowds felt when they heard the words of Jesus to the man who had become rich beyond the dreams of avarice – at their expense. Untouchable? They would have dismembered him.

But Jesus was totally in command. Knowing that, Zacchaeus blundered down, led Jesus to his home and graciously made Him welcome. The crowd? Whatever their prejudices urged them to do, they followed. Grace is a powerful force. And it is contagious. There was no Truth and Reconciliation Commission, though one might have helped. Zacchaeus, too, caught the grace. He offered to give half his wealth to the poor and to use the other half to make restitution to all the people he had defrauded. And there would have been a great many of those! In doing this, he went way beyond what the law required him to do.

'Jesus said to him, "Today salvation has come to this house. . . . For the Son of Man came to seek and to save what was lost." ' Luke 19:9, 10, TNIV.

Whatever else we could say about Zacchaeus, at least he wanted to see Jesus! His need was as great as that of Bartimaeus. His wealth had not brought him happiness. He was despised and hated. An outcast. Lost – and he wanted to be found.

Jesus came to save *the lost*. The New Testament word 'lost' does not mean 'damned'. It means *in the wrong place*. The Far Country, away from the Father's House, is always the wrong place. Jesus says, 'My Father's house has plenty of room; if that were not so, would I have told you that I am going there to prepare a place for you?' John 14:2, TNIV.

To take Zacchaeus to His Father's house, Jesus first had to join him in his house. To do so He had to ignore the wrath and cut through the prejudice of the religious people.

Every barrier is dissolved in Christ. No individuals or groups are irreconcilable. No walls, however historic, are too high or too thick to be broken down. (Ephesians 2:11-22.)

Through the manner of Jesus' birth and death, God identified with the poor, the marginalised and the victims of injustice. And He did so *literally*. Jesus was born in an animal's feeding trough. When He was presented for circumcision His parents gave two pigeons – the gift presented by the poorest class of people. Jesus 'preached the Gospel to the poor'; it was the central part of His mission and was always going to be (Matthew 11:5; Luke 4:16-19; Isaiah 61:1, 2). Jesus lived among the poor. The poor were drawn to Him. Jesus said, 'The foxes have holes and the birds nests: but the Son of Man has nowhere to call his own.' (Matthew 8:20; Luke 9:58, paraphrased.)

When Jesus went to Calvary, all He possessed was what He stood up in: and, on the cross, He was stripped of even that.

Chapter *14*

Do All Roads Lead to God?

She was silenced by rational argument. But Sharon's silence was the silence of white-hot wrath. I could tell that a devastating riposte was coming. After a few taut moments, she said:

'You *are* wrong! You know why? What you say is *politically incorrect!* It has to be. *All* roads lead to God. *All* religions are pathways to God. They each reveal something about what God is like and, taken together, make a composite picture. Christ is no more or less divine than Krishna, Mohammed or Zoroaster. . . .'

Well, it's a point of view. And a very attractive one. There is an inclusivity about it that commends it to a temperament conditioned by tolerance. Many people try hard to stay abreast of the latest Government take on what is 'correct' and 'acceptable' in viewpoint and behaviour.

These days there is a sense in which it is no longer what is true that is important. It is what is fashionable, what is 'cool'. Comparative Religion has replaced Theology in many universities, and is more likely than Bible Knowledge to be taught in schools.

Knowing *Jesus* Knowing *God*

While the study of comparative religion might be an admirable concession to a world which has become a 'global village', it is wrong to assume that it leads to the conclusions drawn by my articulate friend.

Sharon knew that for herself by the next time I came across her. Was she won over by my eloquence? *In my dreams!*

At our next encounter, Sharon was arguing from a very different perspective. *She* was telling *me* the reasons why all religions could not possibly lead to God. Indeed, she made the case that *no* religion did. The total dissimilarity among world religions was what she had learned from her Comparative Religion course. She had found no evidence whatever that all religions were variations on a common theme.

'The most radical dissimilarity among world religions is in their teaching about God,' she told me.

'Islam's "god",' Sharon said, 'is singular and personal. Hinduism's "god" is plural and impersonal. Christianity's God is Creator of all things; the Word made flesh, who came to live among us. The divine in Buddhism is neither personal nor creative. . . .'

Before I had finished nodding my head, Sharon had thought of other dissimilarities: 'Judaism prohibits all attempts to make images of God. Hinduism depends on images. Islam permits a man to have four wives; Christianity prescribes one only. . . .'

After pausing for breath, Sharon thought of other differences: 'Buddhism says there is no forgiveness and no involvement by God in human life. Life's ultimate goal, according to Buddhism, is extinction – *Nirvana* – achieved by the Buddha after no fewer than 547 births. Think of that: 547 *Groundhog* lifetimes! The goal of life for Christians, by contrast, is to know God, have a personal relationship with Him, and enjoy Him forever. . . .'

A course in Comparative Religion had, unusually, led my friend to apply the same critical analysis to all religions. In consequence

Do All Roads Lead to God?

she had achieved a higher estimation of the Person and significance of Jesus Christ.

One common denominator Sharon had found among most religions was a belief in the need of self-redemption: the importance of achieving or deserving 'salvation' (variously understood) by dint of hard slog; personal effort; paddling one's own canoe. Buddhism, for example, began like the story of the lost son. However, in Buddhism's version, when the errant son returned to the father's house he was made to work off the penalty for his misdeeds by years of hard labour. The key concept was *karma* (atoning for/paying off your guilt).

In world religions other than those based on what Christians understood as 'sacred Scripture', redemption was achieved by behavioural reformation, performance. Outside the Bible, more especially the New Testament, there was no trace of the all-gracious, all-forgiving Father God. The concept of *karma* was a million miles from the grace of Christ (forgiveness freely given).

Not just the notions of 'god' were radically dissimilar among world religions, but their understanding of the process of 'salvation' (if any).

Sharon had especially reacted against the postmodern assumption that all 'truth' was equally good, equally bad, because equally meaningless. This assumption underlay much of the discussion occasioned by her comparative religion studies. She concluded that the cynicism so evident in contemporary society was grounded in it.

To these differences between world religions could be added more. The majority of religions view history as a cycle endlessly and meaninglessly repeated: birth, growth, decay, death. By contrast, the Judaeo-Christian view of history was as a journey or pilgrimage: not meaningless, but a meaningful movement towards a goal.

Unique in the Christian understanding of history was the belief that God intervened in it. In the history of the Jewish people, at a time and in a manner prophesied in the Old Testament Scriptures, 'the Word was made flesh': God, the Creator, became flesh and blood and moved into our neighbourhood. His life among us not only demonstrated what God had always been like; it taught us how God regarded pain, suffering, injustice and poverty. More than that, it taught us how a truly righteous life should be lived, and how One who had that life, through a coalition between the religious and political authorities, could be unjustly executed by the most demeaning and painful mode of execution known then or since. Finally, it taught us how – through His conquest of death – sin, death, suffering and injustice would eventually be ended and an all-righteous, everlasting Kingdom of God introduced.

Sharon concluded that all religion is man going in search of God. For that reason she arrived at the belief that religion, *all* religion, must fail. Mere mortals could not find God, however long they looked.

She was right, of course. We don't find God. We, initially, meet God through His self-disclosure. In other words, we don't find God. God finds us.

And He finds us through His ultimate self-disclosure in the Person of Jesus.

All religions do not lead to God. None of them do.

In Jesus God comes to us, His self-centred creatures.

Chapter *15*

God in the Neighbourhood

'The Word became flesh and blood, and moved into the neighborhood. We saw the glory with our own eyes, the one-of-a-kind glory, like Father, like Son, Generous inside and out, true from start to finish.' John 1:14, MGE.

A workman slipped from his scaffolding and plummeted earthward. His fall was broken by the canopy on a street-side stall. Then, stunned and confused, he slipped off the canvas. He hit the pavement with a thud.

A crowd gathered. A policeman walked importantly to the scene. Seeing the prostrate figure on the pavement, he asked, 'What's going on here? What's it all about?' In a daze, but beginning to recover, the workman said, 'Don't ask me! I only just arrived!'

That's how it is with us. We're comparative newcomers. We don't have a practice-run at life. We're not born with answers to such questions as, 'What's it all about?' We have to discover the answers for ourselves.

Knowing *Jesus* Knowing *God*

The fact of the world indicates an outside cause. Time plus Matter plus Chance do not make a world.

From the fact of human life we may infer that the Cause is not only intelligent, but personal.

The fact that humans have a conscience indicates that the personal Cause is concerned about right conduct, and values such as truth, beauty and goodness may have their origin in Him.

The fact that no nation in the world has lived without belief in God may suggest that God wants our worship.

However, that is as far as rationality takes us, because He remains an unknown God. While the many world religions reflect man's centuries of speculations about God, they only complicate the picture by portraying Him in radically different ways. It is unlikely that man will progress any further than that toward God because of his nature. Unless, that is, God chooses to reveal Himself to man. . . .

The Bible's portrayal of the nature of man is not complimentary, but it rings true. Man is not an earnest seeker after God: quite the contrary. (Colossians 1:21.) His 'heart is deceitful above all things' and all but 'beyond cure' (Jeremiah 17:9, TNIV). Far from searching for truth, his corrupt state conditions him to 'suppress' it (Romans 1:18, TNIV). The 'verdict' on man: faced with a choice, he naturally inclines toward darkness rather than light (John 3:19).

If the point of religion is man's search for God – and it would appear that it is – that search will not be successful, if only because of man's corrupt condition. What man needs is not *a religion*, but *a revelation*. The Bible does not pretend that man is searching for God. *It reveals God's search for man.*

The Bible's supreme revelation is God in the Person of Jesus Christ. Corrupt human nature, however, means that, even faced with that supreme revelation, man does not welcome the best even when he comes across it. His instinct is to destroy what is

God in the Neighbourhood

best because it makes him feel small, deficient and outclassed.

The assertion that 'our hearts are in the right place' – that at heart we are all decent types – may be true in the biological sense only. In the moral sense it is belied by the climb of the crime statistics. 'There is no one righteous, not even one; . . . there is no one who seeks God. All have turned away. . . .' (Romans 3:10-12, TNIV.) The hold that sin has on man is like an addiction (see John 8:34, MGE).

The greatness of God and the corrupt nature of man are two major reasons why the all-religions-lead-to-God assertion is a fallacy.

Christianity, properly understood, is not a religion: *us searching for God.* It is a rescue revelation: *God coming to us.*

Agnostic philosopher Herbert Spencer argued that the Infinite could not be known by the finite. There is some validity in that argument, but it is flawed. What if the Infinite should find a way of revealing Himself to the finite? How would that work?

Through God-inspired Scriptures, perhaps?

What if the Infinite cared so deeply about the finite, and wanted so desperately to rescue finite man from his corruption, that He was prepared to come and live as a Man among men? The ultimate self-revelation of God?

Christianity is the only faith that claims that He has done precisely that.

After two thousand years of direct intervention and prophetic revelation, the Jewish nation was convinced that there was one God, no contest.

Politically and culturally, the times favoured God's rescue plan. The Greek language and culture were universal. The extent of the Roman Empire's control had established an unprecedented, widespread peace over territories formerly occupied in tribal conflict. The network of Roman roads was the basis of a communication system which greatly helped the spread of ideas.

Knowing *Jesus* Knowing *God*

Ever heard the expression, 'the fullness of time'? It was first used by Christ's great champion, Paul, to refer to the unique collection of circumstances present at the turn of the eras: eras which, much later, became known as BCE (Before the Christian Era) and CE (the Christian Era), and before that, BC (Before Christ) and AD (Anno Domini: 'the Year of Our Lord'). He used it in this context: 'But when the fulness of the time was come' 'God sent his Son, born of a woman, subject to the law. God sent him to buy freedom for us . . . so that he could adopt us as his very own children' (Galatians 4:4, 5, KJV and NLT).

It was through His Son Jesus Christ that the Infinite made Himself known to the finite. As important as making Himself known, God's Son was the means of man's rescue. He was called Jesus ('God the Rescuer') or Emmanuel ('God among us').

When the stage of history was set, God came in Jesus so that all men and women could see:

- That God is, and who He is;
- That God speaks, and what He says;
- That God cares, and how far that caring goes.

To quote Paul again, in Jesus God 'emptied himself, taking the form of a slave, being born in human likeness. And being found in human form, he humbled himself and became obedient to the point of death – even death on a cross' (Philippians 2:7, 8, NRSV).

God 'emptied Himself' first at Bethlehem, then at Golgotha.

At Bethlehem, and subsequently in the life and ministry of Jesus, God revealed Himself to man so that man need never fumble through the dark alleys of religion in a vain search for God.

At Golgotha, God, through Jesus, made possible Planet Earth's rescue.

The Way, the Truth and the Life is Jesus. He is the One Road to God.

Chapter *16*

One Way to God

Jesus was both
- God's perfect revelation of Himself to man, and,
- God's rescue mission for man.

'God sent him to buy freedom for us . . . so that he could adopt us as his very own children' (Galatians 4:5, NLT).

The Christian claim that God intervened in history, for the purposes of
- revealing God perfectly and
- rescuing man, set Christianity apart from every other religion.

Jesus did not come to point the way to God. He came to *be* the Way to God. He said that Himself, in those terms (John 14:6).

In Jesus, God comes to us. By coming to us, Jesus became our One Way to God. That Way potentially brings a totally new life to us.

Paul, the great champion of Jesus in the decades following His resurrection, explained the whole thing. 'God was in Christ,

Knowing *Jesus* Knowing God

reconciling the world to himself, no longer counting people's sins against them. . . . For God made Christ, who never sinned, to be the offering for our sin, so that we could be made right with God through Christ' (2 Corinthians 5:19, 21, NLT).

The consequences of our taking Christ's one Way to God? 'This means that anyone who belongs to Christ has become a new person. The old life is gone; a new life has begun!' (2 Corinthians 5:17, NLT.)

Time for a recap?

I think so.

- Why do we need rescuing?
- How does the adoption process work that leads to new life?

Our lives are in a mess. Our society is in a mess. Our world is in a mess. The mess has many symptoms, but one cause. That cause is sin. Sin is a consequence of living in God's world as if there were no God. Through Jesus, God showed us His better way. God's law shows us that we need that better way, and, like a mirror, reveals what is wrong and why rescue is imperative.

Jesus showed us what God is like by His incomparable life.

Jesus made it possible for us to be put right with God – *and* receive new life – by His sacrificial death on the cross.

On the cross Jesus, the God-Man, took responsibility for human sin in its totality. 'For Christ also suffered once for sins, the righteous for the unrighteous, to bring you to God . . .' (1 Peter 3:18, TNIV). 'This is love: not that we loved God, but that he loved us and sent his Son as an atoning sacrifice for our sins' (1 John 4:10, TNIV).

The key word in understanding the mission of Jesus is *reconciliation*.

- By repenting of our sins (the mess we are in), we are reconciled to God and become His adopted children.
- By being reconciled to God through Jesus we become part

One Way to God

of God's rescue plan for the world. 'God has given us this task of reconciling people to him' (2 Corinthians 5:18, NLT). Those who receive God's grace become gracious. Those who are reconciled become reconcilers.

Once we grasp that, we realise that religion, too often, is part of the problem. Too often religion – and its toxic mix with politics and economics – defines the battle lines of the groups who need to be reconciled.

It is important to see the Person of Jesus as apart from religion. The Pharisees, rightly, identified Jesus as the enemy of religion. Jesus, not institutional religion, is the Way, the Truth and the Life. Jesus, not any religion, is the only Way to the Father. Salvation is not in the gift of any religion, institution, or priesthood. It comes to us when we reach out with the empty hand of faith to Jesus. We receive salvation and new life from Jesus.

Accept no substitute for the One who died as your Substitute. Those who are reconciled to God take up God's work of reconciling men and women, girls and boys, to Him. But in no sense do they become God's deputies or stand-ins.

No religion or religious institution or hierarchies of institutions are the way to salvation. The way to salvation is Jesus, who died for our sins. Primarily we relate to Him, and not just at the time of our first approach. We relate to Him at every step of the way. And – praise God! – *He* relates to us.

Jesus cared enough to die for you. *Jesus* rose from the grave – conquered death – as a pledge of your future. *Jesus* is the One who wants to share His life with you.

Christianity is right to teach that our main problem is sin, but wrong if it suggests that it can dispense forgiveness and salvation. Only God in Jesus does that.

Chapter **17**

Dressed for the Banquet

To illustrate how we are saved from sin, inspired writers use word pictures. One used frequently is 'the garments of salvation'. Old Testament prophets use it. Jesus uses it and tells two banquet stories to ensure that we understand it. Finally, at the very end of the Bible, there is the picture of the great, international multitude of the saved of every age, standing before God's throne singing His praises and all 'wearing white robes' (Revelation 7:9, 10).

Specifically, they are praising God for His rescue operation through Jesus ('the Lamb'). As a result of this, the tattered rags of their fancied goodness are covered by the gleaming, unblemished robes of Christ's perfect righteousness.

The Bible verses that mention this robe of salvation reference Isaiah's prophecy, chapter 61, verse 10. There the prophet says,
'I delight greatly in the LORD;
my soul rejoices in my God.
For he has clothed me with garments of salvation
and arrayed me in a robe of his righteousness' (TNIV).

Dressed for the Banquet

When a later prophet uses that word picture, the setting is a courtroom. An imposing courtroom, then.[1] The judge is impressive. The court is in session. The chief prosecutor is very vocal. But is there a Counsel for the defence?

The shocker for the first readers of this prophecy, the generation immediately following the Babylonian exile, is the man in the dock.

In the dock is the widely respected High Priest, Joshua, known by everyone. But they have never seen him looking like this. In place of the imposing, high-priestly regalia are the stinking rags of a vagrant.

Shock. Horror. How can this be? This is the spiritual leader of the nation who officiates in the rebuilt temple. This man has the awesome privilege, once a year, of being the ultimate intermediary between the people and God.

Hey! What *is* going on here?

He, above all people, must be squeaky clean. But look at him! He's emitting the stomach-churning stench from the filthy rags of a downmarket druggy.

Hearts sink. The High Priest is not just unfit for the presence of God. He's unfit for anybody's presence. He's unfit for purpose. And yet . . . and yet . . . if that is the way the high priest appears through the eyes of God – *and it is!* – then what chance do the ordinary people have?

The judge is 'the Angel of the Lord'.

To his right hand, the prosecuting counsel, 'the accuser, Satan', has much to say. And all of it cakes layer after layer of shame and scandal on the already sorry figure of the accused: Joshua, the High Priest.

After an encounter with God in a vision, Isaiah says: 'It's all over! I am doomed, for I am a sinful man' (Isaiah 6:5, NLT).

When Peter met Jesus 'he fell to his knees before Jesus and said, "O Lord, please leave me – I'm too much of a sinner to be around you" ' (Luke 5:8, NLT).

So spare a thought for Joshua. How can a sinful man *ever* be acceptable to the all-righteous God?

A change of scene.

The Bible pictures God's final intervention in history as a Great Banquet. Jesus uses the picture twice.[2]

Invitations are sent out. However, at this stage, the date and time of the banquet are not announced.

Time elapses to allow for preparations to be made. Banquets last for days – and the whole community is invited. There are no watches. Time is more elastic.

When the preparations are complete the servants who have issued the invitations are sent out again. Their message: 'All is ready! It's time to sit down to the banquet!'

Jewish people understood that the Great Banquet was a Messianic occasion. They would have realised that Jesus was using the picture to talk about His coming Kingdom. Jesus told the banquet story twice.

In the version recorded by Luke (14:15-24) the invitations are issued. But when the servants go to the invitees a second time to say, 'The banquet is ready!' events take a surprising turn: 'they all alike began to make excuses' (vs. 18).

All the excuses are, for different reasons, implausible. Jesus is using humour. The third excuse, in particular, would provoke laughter.

- 'I have just bought a field and must inspect it. Please excuse me.' Fields are inspected *before* purchase. Otherwise how can the purchaser know what price to offer?
- 'I have bought five pairs of oxen, and I want to try them out. Please excuse me.' Oxen are tried out *before* purchase. Everyone knows that.
- 'I now have a wife so I can't come!' This is not the first strike

Dressed for the Banquet

of a 'She Who Must Be Obeyed'. It's an inappropriate (and therefore comic) reference to a law in Deuteronomy (24:5) that permitted newly-married males to be excused from military service. But this is a banquet, not a military campaign. Wives are welcome.

The servant reports the excuses back to his master. To illustrate that God's purposes can be resisted but not thwarted, Jesus has the master send his servant out a third time. The outsiders normally overlooked are invited; and a greater note of urgency spikes the invitation. Those who have made excuses are taken at their word. No pressure.

Does something disturb us about this? When God throws a party, would we not prefer Him to be fashionably inclusive? Would we not prefer the original invitees to be given a second chance rather than be taken at their word?

If that disturbs us, we shall be a great deal more disturbed by this aspect of the story when Jesus tells it in Matthew 22:1-14. Jesus wants us to be grown up about this. Life is not like a game of chess in which the chess pieces are put away in the box for another game tomorrow. Life choices have consequences.

When Jesus tells the story in Matthew's Gospel, the master is a king and the banquet a wedding supper for his son.

For centuries Jews had known that when Messiah came God would throw a great party for them. However, when Messiah came in the Person of Jesus, He was received with indifference, hostility and any number of excuses. When this happens to the king in the story he is 'furious' (vs. 7, NLT). The original invitees, who have taken it for granted that they have an exclusive right to the banquet on their own terms, are again obliged to live with the negative consequences of their negative choices.

The king tells his servants that 'the wedding feast is ready'. Hence they must go out again. This time they must extend the invitation to the riff-raff, hoi polloi, the uttermost, the outermost.

Knowing *Jesus* Knowing **God**

The 'whosoever will' might come.

We would prefer to hear that God loves us as we are and doesn't want us to change. In fact, of course, when the blind and lame came to Jesus, He did not say, 'You're all right as you are': He healed them. The love of Jesus reached the prostitutes and extortioners where they were, but His love refused to let them stay as they were. Jesus didn't leave them where He found them. Love wants the best for the beloved.

In the second telling of the story, the not-everybody-makes-it point comes over even more strongly. After all, initially, the invitees had ignored the invitation and continued about their business. They had 'paid no attention' to the king's heralds. When they received the second 'come and dine' invitation, they had mistreated and murdered the heralds. That is when the King became politically incorrect. He obliged the original invitees to live with their choices: and instead invited those they might have despised to take their places.

We're not really comfortable with this. We might prefer to hear that God loves people so much that they *all* end up at the banquet, regardless of their choices and priorities.

But Jesus has still not finished His story.

All who are invited receive the invitation because of the King's grace. No one is invited because he has a right to be there.

The King graciously issues the final, urgent message, 'Everything is ready. Come to the banquet!'

Grace gathers them into the banquet and grace provides the banquet absolutely free.

By a final act of grace the king provides free, beautiful robes (wedding garments) for all the guests to wear. That way the poor do not have to be ashamed of their rags and the rich cannot put on a show because of their richly embroidered gowns. 'For it is by grace you have been saved. . . .'[3]

Dressed for the Banquet

In the story told by Jesus, one person refuses the wedding garment in the belief that his one-hundred-percent homemade outfit is good enough.

'Friend,' says the King, 'how did you get in here without wedding clothes?'[4]

The guest must be thinking that if his garments are good enough for him, they have to be good enough for the King. But they are not.

Are we uncomfortable with the strict dress code of the Kingdom? After all, this man has not made excuses. He has not pleaded other commitments. He has not put the claims of business, novelty and domestic things ahead of God.

But he is thrown out!

What has he done?

Simply this.

He has pushed his way in and, in response to the offer of the free wedding garment provided by the King, he has said: 'Don't want it. Don't need it. Got plenty of my own. This is my best and it will have to be good enough for the King.'

But it is not. It never is.

He has accepted the invitation. But he has not accepted the basis of the invitation. *Grace.*

He has spurned the 'robe of righteousness' (Isaiah 61:10) and turned up togged out in his own righteousness. 'We are all infected and impure with sin. When we display our righteous deeds, they are nothing but filthy rags' (Isaiah 64:6, NLT). So much for man-made righteousness!

That takes us back to the courtroom where Joshua the High Priest stands in filthy rags. He is unfit for the presence of God. And there is Satan dishing the dirt on him.

Does Joshua have a defence counsel?

Yes-s-s-s!

Knowing Jesus Knowing God

'And the LORD said to Satan, "I, the LORD, reject your accusations. . . . This man is like a burning stick that has been snatched from the fire." '

The Lord orders that Joshua's filthy robes be taken from him, and a new garment provided. 'See, I have taken away your sins. . . .'[5]

The only garments in which Joshua could stand before a holy God were the garments of the One who came to take away the sins of the world.

When the lost son returned home to the Prodigal Father, penitent but with the stink of the pigsty about him, the Father said, 'Bring the best robe and put it on him. . . .'

The wedding garment is 'woven in the loom of heaven [and] has in it not one thread of human devising'.[6]

The wedding garment – the only basis for our salvation – is the robe of Christ's perfect righteousness.

[1] Zechariah chapter 3.
[2] Luke 14:15-24 and Matthew 22:1-14.
[3] Ephesians 2:8-10.
[4] Matthew 22:11-14.
[5] Zechariah 3:2-4, NLT.
[6] Ellen G. White, *Christ's Object Lessons*, p. 311.

*Chapter **18***

God Still Does Wrestling

Question. How can a flawed human ever be acceptable to an all-righteous God?

Answer. By being covered by the flawless righteousness of Jesus, 'the Lamb of God' who 'takes away the sin of the world'.

Question. How does that work?

Answer. Through the Cross and after a person acknowledges that he is incapable of saving himself – deserving salvation – even by the best behaviour of which he is capable.

'All of us have become like one who is unclean, and all our righteous acts are like filthy rags; we all shrivel up like a leaf, and like the wind our sins sweep us away' (Isaiah 64:6).

We cannot deserve salvation by our behaviour. Those who profess to live without sin are mistaken about the nature of sin. To steer Christians away from such delusional thinking, Jesus said that the self-righteous 'will certainly not enter the kingdom of heaven'.[1] He explained that sin involves not just actions, but attitudes and motives. The commandment that outlawed killing

83

people also concerned anger and intention, as well as the act of murder itself. The commandment against adultery involved lustful intentions as well as actions.[2]

Nine different Hebrew words and six Greek words are translated 'perfect' in the King James Version. But not one of them means 'sinless'. When Jesus uses the word *teleios* (translated 'perfect') in the Sermon on the Mount, He is speaking of the 'completeness' and 'wholeness' of the spiritually mature. Spiritual maturity occurs as we co-operate with the Holy Spirit in becoming spiritually mature.

The Christian is involved in a lifelong battle with sin. God's method of leading us towards spiritual maturity does not involve the eradication of our tendency towards sin. It involves the counteraction of sin by divine power through the Holy Spirit.[3]

Trying to achieve salvation through sinless behaviour is an aspect of *religion*. That was why Jesus spoke against *religion* and *religious people*. Too often they were hypocrites. At the very least they were invariably insufferable.[4] 'If we claim we have no sin, we are only fooling ourselves and not living in the truth. . . . If we claim we have not sinned, we are calling God a liar. . . .'[5] 'But if we confess our sins to him, he is faithful and just to forgive us our sins and to cleanse us from all wickedness.'[6]

The people God chooses to work with have always both fascinated and surprised me. In Scripture, as in life, God works with unpromising people who have conspicuous faults. But those *with whom* God works are also the ones *on whom* He works. He works on them as He leads them through the crises of life in the direction of spiritual maturity.

The Book of Genesis is only partly about the beginning of the world. Mostly it is about the beginning of God's plan to rescue the world. Astonishingly, God revealed that plan to four generations of a highly dysfunctional family. Plaster saints are a phenomenon of

God Still Does Wrestling

institutional Christianity: Christianity as a religion. The practice of idealising the life of a person so that s/he appears perfect in retrospect is called *hagiography*. And hagiography is decidedly *not* a feature of the Bible narrative. Far from it! God worked with (and on) real people. The Bible has a warts-and-all approach to history.

Of the hundreds of examples we could take, let's take Jacob, the ancestor of the Israelis.

In the first sentence of His Manifesto of the Kingdom (also known as the Sermon on the Mount) Jesus commented on the blessedness of those who acknowledge their poverty of spirit, adding 'for the Kingdom of Heaven is theirs' (Matthew 5:3, NLT). What He meant was that the crucial step in an individual's salvation experience is when he acknowledges that he is incapable of saving himself. God cannot save the self-reliant, but, crucially, He can work with just about anybody.

Jacob is proof of that.

If ever there were a 'Mr Fix-it', it was he.

Jacob, spoiled by a doting mother, believed that he could make himself the megastar of his generation. He believed that he could do this by exploiting and manipulating others. But there came a time when, to save his life, his fond mother urged him to flee Beersheba – home – and make the journey to her brother's home in Haran. Beersheba is the last place in the deep south of Palestine before you get to Egypt. Jacob's mother was urging him to make a 400-mile journey up the Jordan Valley, over the Hermon Mountains, across to a Syrian settlement on the Euphrates.

God had already revealed an essential part of His rescue plan for the planet to Abraham and Isaac, Jacob's grandfather and father (Genesis 22). He was to reveal more to Jacob on the first night stop-over on his journey to Haran.

Jacob reached the edge of the Wilderness of Judea at the end of the first day of his camel-borne flight. There, weather erosion

Knowing *Jesus* Knowing *God*

had created strange shapes in the limestone rock. The shelves of limestone, in the fading light, may have looked like the lower part of a grand staircase.

When Jacob settled to sleep he must have felt extremely vulnerable, lonely, anonymous and of absolutely no importance. How *does* God relate to lost sons when they have just left the Father's house – and have not the slightest intention of ever returning there?

In God's rescue plan *He* takes the first step. He granted Jacob a theophany in the form of a vision. In it the great limestone shelves were reconfigured as a grand staircase to Heaven. God's attitude to man and the priority of man's salvation are pictured by Heaven's traffic both up and down the staircase. Then God's voice speaks to Jacob.[7]

A theophany is when, in the crises of our lives, God comes up close and personal. In the Bible's description of the vision, one phrase is capable of two interpretations. Bible translators, on the assumption that God is 'up there' and we are 'down here', have favoured '*There above it* [the staircase], stood the LORD. . . .'[8] However, aware that the first phrase is capable of the translation '*There beside him* [Jacob]', they have invariably included a marginal note to the effect that that is an equally valid rendering. That second interpretation is important. In the great crises of our lives God does not address us from the top of an imposing staircase. He comes alongside. A theophany really *is* a close encounter with God.

To that lonely man who had never felt so unimportant, God said he would be the father of descendants through whom the whole world would be blessed. To that vulnerable and homeless man, God promised that the land on which he was lying would become the possession of his descendants. To that man who felt totally alone, God said, 'I am with you and will watch over you wherever you go. . . .'[9]

God Still Does Wrestling

That is what God says to everyone trying to run away from His grace.

When Jacob awoke he said, 'How awesome is this place! This is none other than the house of God;' and he called the place *Bethel* (Hebrew for 'House of God').

Did Bethel change him? Not so as you would notice. Back in Beersheba he had manipulated and exploited his brother Esau and his father Isaac. Four hundred miles north-east in Haran, he attempted similar stratagems against his uncle Laban, soon also to be his father-in-law. However, over the next twenty years God's grace had its effect on Jacob and he was blessed. He became father to a large family and the owner of immense flocks of sheep and herds of cattle. When he asked Laban if he could take his family and flocks back south to the land of his father, he was told, in effect, 'Not on your life! While God is blessing you, I want *my* share of the action!'[10] But Jacob waited on God's timing and the day came when God said, 'Go . . . *and I will be with you*.'[11]

Try to imagine the immense caravan of people, flocks and herds that headed south from Haran. But there was trepidation in Jacob's heart. He had to face up to his past, and Esau had had twenty years to work up his venom. Wisely, he sent a servant ahead, doubtless on a top-of-the-range camel, with a message and a gift for Esau. The arrangement was that the servant should rejoin Jacob and the great caravan somewhere on the long route south.

The servant had had a very long journey. When he rejoined Jacob and the rest of the party, his news was that Esau was not far behind him. Jacob would meet him the following day. Four hundred men accompanied Esau. Jacob, about to face his past, was 'in great fear and distress'.[12]

If Jacob had ever been caught between a rock and a hard place, he was now. He had thought of himself as reliant on his wits thus far. In this crisis they were not going to be enough.

Knowing *Jesus* Knowing *God*

Was it time for another theophany? He hoped so. (Be careful what you hope for, Jacob.)

Jacob did three things. He divided his huge caravan in two, so that if Esau captured one the other might escape. He reminded God of his promises. And then, wisely, he sent a second gift to Esau. Alone, he then withdrew north of the River Jabbok, a tributary of the Jordan. He was between the proverbial 'rock and a hard place' and, perhaps, was creating the circumstances in which he would experience another theophany in which God would reassure him, as he had done at Bethel.

Not all theophanies are the same. God would speak to Moses from a burning bush in the Sinai. To Joshua He would appear as a Soldier. To Isaiah He would appear as an enthroned Monarch.

To Jacob, by contrast, God came – *as a Wrestler?*

Jacob had done battle with self-centredness. He thought of himself as self-reliant, and was proud of his cleverness.

When his entire family and the impedimenta of his wealth had gone south of the Jabbok, and when Jacob was entirely alone, God granted him a One-on-one encounter. And God came as a Wrestler.

In the account Jacob gives it is clear that he surrendered to God. However, he spins the story so that it reads like a victory for him.

The whole point of wrestling is to get a man down, and hold him down until he submits.

Jacob's wrestling bout lasted until dawn. Surely God could have fettled Jacob in no time. He could, but that is not the way God works. He is not a bully-boy Wrestler. In the interests of His people God goes far beyond the Marquess of Queensberry Rules or the Geneva Conventions. God struggles with us when it is the only way in which He can break our stubborn self-reliance. Our salvation is at stake. Only when we surrender do we accept that salvation is entirely in God's gift. Only then can we have the

God Still Does Wrestling

assurance of God's salvation. The self-righteous can 'in no case enter into the kingdom of heaven'.[13] Only those wearing the robe of Christ's perfect righteousness can enter there.[14]

God saves us by His grace, and He wants us to embody graciousness, love, peace, longsuffering, gentleness and all the other fruits of the Spirit.[15] But they arrive, not overnight, but over time as God's Spirit leads us towards maturity.

The following morning Jacob had two souvenirs of his wrestling theophany: a limp, and a new name. His new name was *Israel*, meaning 'he struggles with God'. The new name brought a new status.

The casualty had not, primarily, been a broken hip, but a smashed ego. Jacob called the place of his second theophany '*Peniel* [the face of God], saying, "It is because I saw God face to face, and yet my life was spared." '[16]

The post-*Peniel* Jacob is very different from the pre-*Peniel* Jacob. When we surrender to God we acknowledge that we can do nothing to help ourselves. We also acknowledge that we have a Captain who has never lost a battle. As long as our eyes are upon Him – *His* grace, *His* righteousness, *His* salvation, *His* power – we can experience assurance. We are acknowledging our poverty of spirit, and the Kingdom of Heaven is ours.

Our trust must be wholly in the merits of the crucified and risen Saviour. If at any stage we look at ourselves, we wonder how we could ever be saved. If at any stage we look at Him, we wonder how we could ever be lost.

It has been suggested that Jacob's overnight wresting bout has an apocalyptic significance.[17] That means that, when the circumstances demand it, God still does wrestling.

Knowing *Jesus* Knowing *God*

[1] Matthew 5:20.
[2] Matthew 5:21-32.
[3] Romans 8.
[4] See Matthew 5:20 and the whole of Matthew 23.
[5] 1 John 1:8, 10, NLT.
[6] 1 John 1:9, NLT.
[7] Genesis 28:10-22.
[8] vs. 13.
[9] Genesis 28:15.
[10] See Genesis 30:25-28.
[11] Genesis 31:3.
[12] Genesis 32:6, 7.
[13] Matthew 5:20, KJV.
[14] Matthew 22:1-14.
[15] See Galatians 5:22-26.
[16] Genesis 32:22-30.
[17] Jeremiah 30:5-7; Ellen G. White, *Patriarchs and Prophets*, p. 201-203.

Chapter *19*

A Ladder Up to Heaven

If we see the Bible narrative as a play, then God may be said to be both Playwright and central Character.

The bottom line of the Bible?

God's perfect revelation is Jesus, and in God there is no unChristlikeness at all. If we think there is, it is because we have misunderstood something. Because Jesus is most clearly revealed in the four Gospel accounts, those Gospels are the lenses through which we must view the rest of Scripture.

The central challenge of the Bible is, 'Taste and see that the LORD is good. . . .'¹ No one else can do the tasting for you. Taste! Read! See! Discover! Adventure! And it will not be long before you find you are adventuring with God.

The Bible is a library of sixty-six books, written over a period of sixteen hundred years. Behind the various authors may be said to be a single divine Author. All sixty-six books are 'God-breathed'. The God who 'breathed' the books, and the human authors who wrote them down, did so to show us a portrait of God.

Knowing *Jesus* Knowing *God*

'Gospel' means 'good news'. And the good news is about God and is meant to be 'useful' to man.[2] In summary, that good news is this:

God is like Jesus and always has been, and Jesus came to open the way to God.

Jacob, you will recall, had a dream of a stairway between Earth and Heaven.[3] On it, going up and down, he saw Heaven's traffic. Jesus claimed to be that stairway.[4]

When Jesus first encountered the disciple Nathaniel, He pronounced him 'a true Israelite' who, by contrast with Jacob, who was the first 'Israelite', possessed 'no guile'.[5] John said of Jesus, 'He did not need man's testimony about man, for he knew what was in a man'.[6] When Jesus gave evidence of His prior knowledge of Nathaniel, the latter exclaimed, 'Rabbi, you are the Son of God – the King of Israel!' Jesus responded, continuing the Jacob allusion, by identifying Himself as the stairway between Earth and Heaven: the One Way to God.[7] A current Bible scholar, commenting on this claim, wrote that Jesus is still 'the meeting point between Heaven's fullness and Earth's need, even in the midst and bustle and noise of our modern world.' Francis Thompson made the same point in his poem 'The Kingdom of God', in which he spoke of 'Jacob's ladder, pitched betwixt Heaven and Charing Cross'.[8]

Man's salvation process, symbolised by the stairway to Heaven, was explained by Christ's great champion Paul in 'possibly the most important single paragraph ever written'.[9]

'But now a righteousness from God, apart from law, has been made known, to which the Law and the Prophets testify. This righteousness from God comes through faith in Jesus Christ to all who believe. There is no difference, for all have sinned and fall short of the glory of God, and are justified freely by his grace through the redemption that came by Christ Jesus. God presented

A Ladder Up to Heaven

him as a sacrifice of atonement, through faith in his blood.'[10]

In that single paragraph the Gospel is tightly packed. To unpack it a little:

- Humans 'of every creed and culture . . . , the immoral and the moralising, the religious and the irreligious, are without any exception sinful, guilty . . . before God' (Stott). That point was made in Romans 1:18-3:20, and is made again in 3:23.
- *'But now'* (vs. 21, KJV) (through Jesus) *'the righteousness of God'* or 'God's way of righteousness' has been revealed. 'After the long dark night the sun has risen, a new day has dawned, and the world is flooded with light.' (Stott.)
- God's righteousness is *apart from law* (vs. 21), but it was not a divine afterthought: it had been foreshadowed in the Old Testament Scriptures. By contrast with the self-righteousness of the religious and the unrighteousness of others, Paul sets the perfect (flawless) righteousness of God revealed in Jesus. This is the new, fresh revelation of the Gospel.
- The really important thing about his perfect righteousness is that, through Christ's death on the Cross, it is available as a gift. Verse 22 says, *'This righteousness from God comes through faith in Jesus Christ to all who believe.'* This is simply sublime and sublimely simple. It comes to those who know they cannot save themselves – and reach out the empty hand of faith to grasp salvation.
- *'. . . for all have sinned and fall short of the glory of God'* (vs. 23). All have forfeited God's approval. There may be 'degrees of sinning': some sinners may be down at the bottom of the mineshaft, while other sinners may be astride the mountain peak. But *all* are unable to touch the stars.
- *'. . . and are justified freely by his grace through the redemption that came by Christ Jesus'* (vs. 24). Yes, there are some tough terms in there.
- There is *justified* for one. It is a term from the law courts of

Knowing *Jesus* Knowing **God**

Paul's day. There were two alternative verdicts that a judge could pronounce: you could be *condemned* or you could be *justified*. If you were *justified*, however, you were far more than declared 'not guilty'. *Justified* meant even more than pardoned, for pardon means 'the remission of a penalty or debt'. *Justified* is better than that. Much better. *Justified* is the bestowal of a righteous status. It is the sinner's reinstatement in the favour and approval of God.

Forgiveness says, 'You may **go**. You have been let off the penalty your sin deserves.'

Justification says, 'You may **come**. You are welcome to all my love and my presence.'

However, while *justified declares* a person righteous, it does not *make* them righteous.

- *Justification* is a new status. *Regeneration* is a new heart. The latter is the work of the Holy Spirit within us. It begins when we are justified. *Regeneration* is a process by which the Holy Spirit leads us on the road to progressive spiritual growth.

Nevertheless, *justification* is a most radical concept and, because it restores us to God's presence, we need to examine its basis:

- *'freely by his grace'* (vs. 24) means that the salvation initiative from beginning to end comes from God. It is an initiative God takes when we are both helpless and hopeless sinners.

- *'through the redemption that came by Christ Jesus'* (vs. 24). The basis on which our righteous God declares the unrighteous to be righteous without compromising His righteousness or condoning unrighteousness – is the Cross. God justifies us because 'Christ died for the ungodly' (Romans 5:6), because *'God presented him [Jesus] as a sacrifice of atonement'* (Romans 3:25). The

A Ladder Up to Heaven

death of Jesus was a sacrificial one.

- The Cross is the basis of *redemption*, too (vs. 24). *Justified* is a term Paul borrowed from the law courts. *Redemption* is a term he borrowed from the market place. In the Old Testament when slaves were bought in order to be set free they were said to be 'redeemed'. Jesus bought us out of a captivity from which we were totally unable to liberate ourselves. The price He paid was Calvary. There *'God presented him* [Jesus] *as a sacrifice of atonement'* (vs. 25).

And *atonement* gives us one final term to unpack. That term is so closely bound up with Calvary that I feel unable to explain it without describing what happened there.

Dramas usually feature a last-minute crucial intervention. The word 'crucial' actually comes from the Latin for 'cross'. It is the Cross that changes everything.

> 'O safe and happy shelter, O refuge tried and sweet.
> O trysting place where Heaven's love and Heaven's justice meet!
> As to the homeless patriarch that wondrous dream was given,
> So seems my Saviour's Cross to me, a ladder up to Heaven.'

Elizabeth Clephane

[1] Psalm 34:8.
[2] 2 Timothy 3:15-17.
[3] See Chapter 18.
[4] John 1:51.
[5] John 1:47, NIV, KJV.
[6] John 2:25.
[7] See John 1:47-51, NLT.
[8] Quoted Bruce Milne, *The Message of John* (IVP), pp. 60, 61.
[9] These words are from Dr Leon Morris, but similar words are used of this passage in the commentaries on Romans by John R. W. Stott and F. F. Bruce.
[10] Romans 3:21-25.

Chapter 20

Were You There?

Roman Governor Pilate pronounced the formula *'Ibis ad crucem'* ('You will go to the cross'). Jesus immediately fell into the custody of a four-man execution squad. Those handpicked, battle-hardened torturers knew all about inflicting pain and ensuring death.

The flagrum

Prior to crucifixion, they whipped Jesus viciously. Jewish rules limited the number of lashes to thirty-nine, but it is unlikely the Romans were bound by that limitation. The *flagrum* used for whipping had long leather thongs of varying lengths, each with sharp, jagged pieces of bone and lead attached to them. In the course of the thirty-nine lashes across the back and legs of the prisoner, the blows would cut through subcutaneous tissue, rendering the back an unrecognisable mass of torn, bleeding flesh. Many did not survive the thirty-nine lashes.

Were You There?

The cross

Crucifixion involved driving seven-inch spikes through both heel bones. Wrought-iron spikes were driven through the front of each wrist, causing the incomplete severing of the median nerve. Because of the prisoner's position, air would be drawn into the lungs, which could not be exhaled. Carbon dioxide would build up in the lungs and the bloodstream. Death came by suffocation. Eventually.

The sham trials

Jesus' body was bleeding and broken *before* He had been crucified. He had taken neither food nor drink since the previous night. His sham trials had occupied most of the night and involved appearances before Annas, Jerusalem's religious 'boss', his son-in-law the High Priest Caiaphas, and a covertly convened caucus of those on the religious Ruling Council who could be depended on to support a call for the execution of Jesus. He had endured a farcical and deeply humiliating appearance before King Herod. His final appearance had been before the Roman Governor, who interrogated Jesus in hearing distance of a drummed-up, bought-and-paid-for ruck of people.

The expedient

Pilate knew Jesus was innocent of all charges, and said so, but, politically vulnerable, he opted for an expedient. The expedient was to give the choice to the mob. They could choose between Jesus and Barabbas. The latter was a murderer whose villainies had been hogging headlines. The Governor told the rabble that they could choose between liberating Jesus or Barabbas. They chose to liberate Barabbas.

That was the juncture when Pilate cravenly sent Jesus for whipping, and from thence to the place of crucifixion. The state He was in after the whipping meant that He was unable on His

Knowing *Jesus* Knowing *God*

own to carry the cross which had been prepared for Barabbas to Golgotha.

Golgotha

Golgotha, a skull-shaped hill, was outside of, but within sight of, the walls of Jerusalem. It was situated where the roads from Joppa and Damascus converged so that the hordes of Jewish pilgrims arriving from the north and west would be obliged to witness the crucifixion of Jesus and of two of the confederates of Barabbas. The liberation of that criminal, and Jesus' death in his place, has been used to illustrate the meaning of Calvary. Jesus died as our Substitute so that we might go free.

'God made him who had no sin to be sin for us, so that in him we might become the righteousness of God' (or 'so that we could be made right with God through Christ').[1]

He was condemned that we might be justified. His was the agony that ours might be the victory. He suffered and died so that all who believe might be covered by the spotless robe of His righteousness.

Three groups

Jesus was in full view of the great Passover multitude during the six hours it took Him to die. But it has been suggested that every human who has ever existed – past, present, future – was there, including you and me.

Among the visible multitude who were looking and straining to hear were three groups: the apathetic, the sympathetic and the hostile.

Of the three groups, the sympathetic was definitely the smallest: a few disciples including John, but mostly women.

Next, perhaps, were the hostiles: the religious establishment and the various vested interest groups there to make sure that He died.

The largest group, almost certainly, were the apathetic: the

Were You There?

Bank Holiday crowd after entertainment, the pilgrims brought to a standstill by the spectacle, and the Roman soldiers who, having 'twisted together a crown of thorns and set it on his head', crucified Him and gambled for His garment, sat down and 'kept watch over him there'.[2]

Seven sentences

In His six hours on the cross, Jesus spoke seven times. No sooner was the instrument of torture and execution savagely jolted into the socket prepared for it in the ground than Jesus cried:

'Father, forgive them, for they do not know what they are doing.'[3]
And Jesus was not just speaking to the crowd about the cross. His cry still echoes. Jesus was interceding for sinners. We have a fundamental problem, and it is sin. Tackling that problem exposes our fundamental need. That need is for more than a change of environment, the fruits of the best education and psychoanalysis, the success of the most idealistic political programme, or for the trappings of religion. The fundamental need of all sinners – *and we are all sinners* – is for forgiveness, and, beyond that, justification.[4]

The criminal crucified on one side of Jesus 'hurled insults at him'. The criminal on the other side defended Jesus and said, 'Jesus, remember me when you come into your kingdom.'

Jesus replied: *'. . . you will be with me in paradise.'*[5]

The criminal to whom Jesus spoke, despite the mess he was in, had his priorities sorted. He did not ask for release from the cross or the removal of his pain. He had faith enough to ask for salvation.

The religious people at the time of Jesus wanted a jack-booted Messiah who could smash the Romans.

The criminal understood what was really on offer. He believed Jesus had a Kingdom to give away. Jesus did not *appear* like that. Faith made the man see Jesus like that. In his last moment he wanted reconciliation – at-one-ment – with God. Alone among that vast crowd that criminal grasped what was happening. In the statement before he had asked his question he had confessed both his own guilt and the innocence of Jesus. Did he recall, however dimly, the Messianic prophecy of Isaiah? *'But he was pierced for our transgressions, he was crushed for our iniquities; the punishment that brought us peace was upon him, and by his wounds we are healed.'*[6] Isaiah had not prophesied a jack-booted Messiah. Religious expectations and political expectations so easily get mixed up. Here was Isaiah's sinless, suffering Messiah who – even here, even now – was sacrificing Himself to win atonement (at-one-ment) for sinners. And the criminal freely confessed his sinner-status.

This criminal had to be saved by grace alone. He couldn't do great works for the Master. But Jesus promised him Paradise. That tells us that, whatever our past, whatever our weakness – when we repent we have a mighty Saviour!

At the foot of the cross, with John and the female disciples, is Mary the mother of Jesus, who is living her worst nightmare.

'When Jesus saw his mother there, and the disciple whom he loved standing near by, he said to his mother, "Dear woman, here is your son," and to the disciple, "Here is your mother."' [7]

Jesus was about a business bigger than creation itself: redemption. The great problem with human saviours who, over the centuries, have established and built up kingdoms, is that they have lost sight of the individual. The King who begins His reign on the cross at Golgotha is different. He has 'all authority in heaven and on earth'[8] but He simultaneously embraces each one of us in a loving commitment. No one is thrust aside.

Jesus values feelings, and the duties of home. The religious people who feel free 'to be saints abroad and devils at home' are implicitly rebuked here. Salvation involves obedience. Obedience is the *fruit* of salvation. The *root* of salvation is a relationship with

Were You There?

Jesus. Fruitless Christianity is rootless Christianity. A relationship with Jesus *must* and *will* make a difference.

'From the sixth hour until the ninth hour [noon until 3pm] *darkness came over all the land. About the ninth hour Jesus cried out in a loud voice . . . "My God, my God, why have you forsaken me?"* '9

The fourth of the seven utterances of Jesus from the cross is the most significant of all. Professor Tom Wright says, 'There the weight of all the world's evil really did converge upon Jesus, blotting out the sunlight of God's love as surely as the light of day was blotted out for three hours. . . . Jesus is "giving His life a ransom for many", and the sin of the "many", which He is bearing, has for the first and only time in His experience caused a cloud to come between Him and the Father.'10

Jesus endured intense physical pain in silence, but when it seemed that the Father forsook Him His heart broke. The real penalty for sin is not death; in the words of John Donne, 'One short sleep past, we wake eternally.'11 The real penalty is separation from God. Hence on the cross, as our Substitute, Jesus had to experience it. He had to know what it was to be forsaken. Because *He* was forsaken, regardless of how we feel, we never are or shall be.

'Jesus said, "I am thirsty." '12

That is the only time when Jesus indicates His physical suffering. Why? If the sinless Christ suffered, is it so strange that sinners should, too? Whatever we suffer, Jesus has been there before us. Suffering is inevitable; misery is optional.

It is, in a sense, an appeal by Jesus to His torturers. In response, a hard-bitten soldier ran to Him with a sponge.

Immediately after that,

*'Jesus said, "It is finished." With that, he bowed his head and gave up his spirit.'*13 No scene in the narratives of all world

religions comes close to this one.

'It is finished.' Three words in English. One word in Greek. A library of significance in any language.

It was a cry of triumph best translated, 'It is accomplished!'[14]

Question. *What* had been accomplished?

Answer. Christ's mission.

Question. And that was?

Answer. • God's character had been fully revealed in Jesus. Clearly, there are no limits to the love of God. No limits at all.

• Man's atonement (at-one-ment with God) had been accomplished. Every repentant sinner might be justified. By the perfect life and death of Jesus, God's Son, the price of sin had been paid.

Christ's righteousness is the righteousness by which we are saved. We cannot work to earn salvation. Our vain, imperfect efforts to do so, along with our sins, must be laid at His feet. It *is* finished. Grasping that will not cut the nerve of effort; but it will make it less anxious. Our strivings will be joyful when we know that we have been accepted.

'Jesus called out with a loud voice, "Father, into your hands I commit my spirit." When he had said this, he breathed his last.'[15]

Early in this chapter we explained that, in crucifixion, death came by suffocation. The first readers of the Gospels would have realised that something supernatural had happened here. No crucified man, in the final stages of his suffering, ever 'called out with a loud voice'. Except, that is, this One.

The final utterance of Jesus was not in the weak voice of a man whose life was ebbing away. It was in the Voice of One who yet had all power. This death was not that of a helpless, broken victim. It was a triumphant King whose mission had been accomplished and who was committing His life into the hands of Heaven.

Were You There?

'Father, into your hands. . . .' Jesus is showing us how to deal with the traumas and sufferings of life: we leave them to God.

Through the triumph of Christ, no failure is final; no Christian ever says 'Goodbye' for the last time. Truth, joy, life itself, may appear overcome, crucified, dead and buried.

But, through Christ, death is not the end of hope.

[1] 2 Corinthians 5:21, NIV, NLT. The best-written and researched narratives of the crucifixion, using all four Gospel accounts and with recourse to the history of the period, were both published at the end of the nineteenth century: E. G. White's *The Desire of Ages* and Alfred Edersheim's *The History of the Messiah*. Both sources are still in print and well worth reading.
[2] Matthew 27:29, 36.
[3] Luke 23:34.
[4] See chapter 19 and Romans 3:21-25.
[5] Luke 23:39-43.
[6] Isaiah 53:5.
[7] John 19:26, 27.
[8] Matthew 28:18.
[9] Matthew 27:45, 46.
[10] Tom Wright, *Matthew for Everyone* (SPCK), vol. 2, p. 190.
[11] John Donne, 'Holy Sonnet 10', *Death, Be Not Proud*, line 13.
[12] John 19:28.
[13] John 19:30.
[14] F. F. Bruce, *The Gospel of John* (Eerdmans), pages 373, 374.
[15] Luke 23:46.

Chapter *21*

Dead, Buried and . . .

Jesus said, 'No one can take my life from me. I sacrifice it voluntarily.'[1] And that was what happened. Jesus gave Himself freely.

The eternal Word, the One who raised the dead, died. To make sure that Jesus and the two criminals were dead, and that their bodies were removed before sunset when the Sabbath began, the execution squad examined the three men. They broke the legs of the two criminals, thus expediting their death, and then removed their bodies. Finding that Jesus was already dead, one of the soldiers pierced Jesus' side with a spear, bringing 'a sudden flow of blood and water'.[2] The witness who saw this, and subsequently wrote it down, could not have understood its significance. That was revealed by modern medicine; 'This is evidence of massive clotting of blood in the main arteries, and is exceptionally strong medical proof of death. . . .' The separation of the blood into clot and serum is one of the surest indications of death.[3]

Two members of the Jewish ruling council, Nicodemus and

Dead, Buried and . . .

Joseph of Arimathea, absent from the caucus meeting that had convened for the 'trial' of Jesus, now sought permission from the Roman Governor to take down His body and bury it. That permission was given. The small group of devastated disciples and family who witnessed the removal of the body must have been astonished at the involvement of two such prominent men. It became apparent that Jesus had had support even among the Jerusalem establishment. Both men would face ostracism by the Annas-Caiaphas political bosses for the stand they took. Nicodemus brought an unnecessarily large quantity of myrrh and aloes to scent the body. Joseph helped him to remove the body to a tomb close by, which he had prepared for himself.[4]

By the time the Sabbath began at sunset on Friday, Jesus was not only dead. He had been buried.

When Pilate had presented Jesus before the mob, he had used the words, 'Behold the Man!' and the mob had cried for Barabbas. The message of Calvary is not just 'Behold your King!' It is 'Behold your God!' The divine grace that can save and redeem Barabbas and the whole world was there expressed. Everything is done for man's salvation, except to force him to accept it. God forces no one.

Three of the four Gospels mention that the mob was given a choice between freeing Jesus and freeing Barabbas. Ancient manuscripts give the full name of the criminal chosen by the mob to be freed instead of Jesus: *Jesus* Barabbas.[5] There is great irony in that the name 'Barabbas' simply means 'son of the father'. Centre stage at the trial of Christ had been two 'sons of the father' – both called Jesus (a common name in first-century Palestine). Later the majority of biblical manuscripts dropped the personal name of Barabbas. You couldn't have a criminal with the same name as Jesus!

But you could!

It makes the point even more powerfully: Jesus died in the

place of the sinner. With Pilate and in front of the mob stood two sons of the father: both men called Jesus, which means 'God to the rescue'. One, a Zealot or freedom fighter, murdered Romans in the vain hope of achieving a man-made salvation for those who shared his religion. The other, having lived a perfect life, loved, suffered and died graciously to gift His life for the salvation of sinners.

The body in Joseph's new tomb – sealed and guarded by soldiers – was that of Jesus, the flawless Saviour. He was taking Barabbas's place – and ours.

It is, apparently, possible to conspire against the sinless Son of the Father, the Prince of Life, subject Him to the most hideous judicial murder ever devised, and encase His body in a tomb, with a stone estimated to have been between one-and-a-half and two tons in weight blocking the entrance.[6] You can also seal it and post an armed guard – a sixteen-man Roman security detachment – to guard the entrance. But can you keep Him there?

The size of the stone, the use of a Roman seal and the military detachment indicate that the Jewish (and, therefore, Roman) authorities were nervous about something. No one expected a resurrection, of course. The ancient world knew that resurrection did not and could not happen. Certainly the disciples knew that. Following the crucifixion, the disciples were broken, angry and disillusioned. They experienced an horrific 'crisis of faith'. 'They had backed a loser and all they wanted to do was to go away and hide and forget all about the fiasco.'[7]

But if He had been who He claimed to have been – the Prince of Life, the Creator – would mountains piled on mountains over Joseph's tomb have been sufficient to keep Him there?

If first-century Christians invented the story of the resurrection of Jesus, would they have given the starring role to a woman – let alone a woman like Mary Magdalene?

The weeping women, who discovered that the stone had been

Dead, Buried and . . .

removed and that the tomb was empty, related to the discovery as to the final indignity, the ultimate affront and proof that even grief could be violated. And, following their encounter with the risen Christ, when the women related their story, the male disciples 'did not believe the women, because their words seemed to them like nonsense'.[8]

Later on Resurrection Sunday, when the risen Christ caught up with two male disciples en route to Emmaus, He saw that they were in the grip of despair. They were preoccupied with the crucifixion of Jesus, and explained, '. . . but we had hoped that he was the one who was going to redeem Israel.'[9] By the time they realised to whom they were speaking, Jesus had left them. Then 'They got up and returned at once to Jerusalem.'

By the time they arrived at the disciples' upper-room hideaway, they learned that Jesus had spoken to Peter. While they were all together 'Jesus himself stood among them and said to them, "Peace be with you." ' But they 'were startled and frightened, thinking they saw a ghost.'[10]

The one disciple who was absent on the occasion, and who was still giving tongue to his doubts a week later, has been given the label 'Doubting Thomas'. The truth is that all the disciples doubted until they actually encountered Jesus Himself.

The only exception may have been John.[11] He, with Peter, was part of the group that initially disbelieved the women. However, struck by the women's assertion that the tomb was empty, Peter and John ran to investigate. John, the younger man, arrived first at the mouth of the tomb but did not enter. On arrival Peter blundered past him, entered and discovered that the tomb was indeed empty. But Peter 'walked away puzzled, shaking his head'.[12] John walked into the tomb and saw what Peter saw, but 'believed'. The accounts refer to the tidy, orderly state in which Jesus had folded the grave clothes. Recognition of something Jesus had done may have been among the reasons why John was the first male disciple to move towards belief.

What did Peter and John do following the discovery of the empty tomb? 'Then they went home.'[13] No sudden jumps of joy, then! The Gospel account based most closely on Peter's testimony suggests that, when the two Emmaus disciples arrived back at base, 'no one believed them'![14]

No wonder, then, that when the risen Jesus appeared to the disciple group, minus Thomas, He said, 'Why are you troubled, and why do doubts rise in your minds? . . . It is I myself! Touch me and see; a ghost does not have flesh and bones, as you see I have.'[15]

Jesus had already taken two of them on a whistle-stop tour through the Old Testament, explaining 'what was said in all the Scriptures concerning himself'.[16]

Jesus still had to work to remove residual doubts. He asked if there was anything to eat. When they came up with broiled fish, he sat in front of them all and ate it, thus helping to dispel any lingering concern that He was 'a ghost'.[17]

After that, the risen Christ 'opened their minds so they could understand the Scriptures'. Having done so, He gave them a more in-depth, exhaustive tour of the Messianic passages of the Old Testament.[18]

As mentioned, Thomas was absent. When he rejoined the disciple group in the course of the ensuing week, heard what had happened and saw the glow on the faces of his friends, he made his classic statement: 'I won't believe it unless I see the nail wounds in his hands, put my fingers into them, and place my hand into the wound in his side.'[19]

Thomas has had a hard time from preachers. Some suggest that he was semi-detached from the disciple group for fear of Jewish reprisals. That does not stack up. In the past, Thomas had appeared fearless of death. Eight days after Jesus' appearance to the disciples, they were *all* still holed up for fear of the Jewish

Dead, Buried and . . .

authorities.[20] Others have suggested that Thomas's whole attitude to the mission of Jesus was characterised by doubt. To the contrary. On the night of the arrest of Jesus it was Philip who cast doubt on His divinity. Thomas, by contrast, merely showed his usual propensity for wanting everything 'clear and sorted'. Jesus, always tolerant of questions, rewarded Thomas with one of the most powerful and clear statements of mission.[21]

In His teaching Jesus made a distinction between *doubt* and *unbelief*. Doubt could be a process of honest questioning before reaching a firm conclusion on which faith could be built. At worst, doubt was, 'Can't believe'; but unbelief was, 'Won't believe'. Doubt was, at least, looking for light. And that was Thomas all through. Call him dogged in his quest for understanding. Even a bit donkey-like. But when Jesus said, 'Anyone who has seen me has seen the Father', Thomas accepted it.

In *Mere Christianity* C. S. Lewis asserted that the position of both a Christian and an atheist in the faith-doubt spectrum has a lot to do with their prevailing mood. 'Now that I am a Christian,' wrote Lewis, 'I do have moods in which the whole thing looks very improbable: but when I was an atheist I had moods in which Christianity looked terribly probable.' He urged mastery of our mutinous moods, concluding, 'Unless you teach your moods "where they get off", you can never be either a sound Christian or even a sound atheist, but just a creature dithering to and fro, with its beliefs really dependent on the weather and the state of its digestion.'

Thomas was not more fearful or more doubting than the others. He was a bit of a pessimist, but whatever we doubt about Thomas, we are not free to doubt his love for Jesus.[22]

The fact that Thomas was expecting the worst did not make it easier to handle when it happened. Gethesemane. The arrest. The overnight sham trials. Then Golgotha. Whatever Thomas had expected, his expectations stopped short of that.

Knowing *Jesus* Knowing *God*

Could it be that Golgotha was just too much for Thomas? Did its traumas entirely overwhelm him? Was his decision to sit out the trauma in isolation from the group his biggest mistake? Did he go solitary when togetherness was most at a premium?

Resurrection rumours reached Thomas wherever he had chosen to work through his trauma. When he rejoined the disciple group, the shining faces he saw and the testimonies he heard may have added a feeling of exclusion to his trauma. Hence his strong statement, 'Unless I see . . . I will not believe. . . .'

A week after the resurrection, Jesus returned to the disciple group which, by then, included Thomas. Was that to tick off Thomas? Far from it. It was to show that the Lord did not neglect His friends. It may also have been because there were doubts in the group as a whole. Thomas may have been more vocal than the rest. He refused to say that he believed when he did not.

When Jesus returned to the group and offered His wounds for the inspection of Thomas, we discover what Thomas's tough talk amounted to. The sight of the Saviour's wounds was enough to call forth the most sublime affirmation of the deity of Jesus in the New Testament: *'My Lord and my God!'*[23]

The Gospel of John, which is the source of this account, is more than an eye-witness narrative. It has a purpose, spelled out in its opening verses, and it has a structure. The opening verse contains the assertion that Jesus was God. The subsequent chapters contain the 'signs' (evidence) that proved the assertion to be true, the final 'sign' being the resurrection.

In what was meant to be the conclusion of John's account, the author admits that many 'miraculous signs . . . are not recorded in this book'. Then the narrator states that the reason for the inclusion of the 'miraculous signs' than had been described was that 'you may believe that Jesus is the Christ, the Son of God, and that by believing you may have life in his name'.[24]

John's Gospel begins with an assertion of the deity of Jesus.

Dead, Buried and . . .

As the narrative of the 'signs' proceeds, Jesus is called by a number of titles: Master, Teacher, Lord.

The 'bottom line' of John's Gospel is John 20:28. In response to the urging of Jesus that Thomas should 'stop doubting and believe', Thomas utters the punchline of the whole narrative: *'My Lord and my God!'* Are Thomas's words all the more significant because of who he was – the most reflective and quizzical of the disciples?

One writer dismisses Thomas as 'muddled and confused'. Another states that he 'stumbled his way to belief'.

No.

Thomas did not stumble. He leapt. The sight of the wounds of Jesus was enough. His doubts dissolved. The trauma of his grief evaporated. His heart all but punched its way through his ribcage. His words affirmed salvation's bottom line. His doubts had been a process by which he had become sure. Thomas needed everything to be 'clear and sorted'. And, with regard to the resurrection and many other things, he was.

Thomas grasped that the resurrection was not some alien power bursting into God's world. It was what happened when God Himself, the Creator, came to heal and restore His world – and was done to death by evil men.

Knowing Jesus *Knowing* God

[1] John 10:18, NLT.

[2] John 19:31-34.

[3] Dr E. Symes Thompson, *On the Physical Cause of the Death of Christ*, cited Michael Green, *The Empty Cross of Jesus* (1984), pp. 92, 93.

[4] John 19:38-42.

[5] TNIV Matthew 27:16 follows the ancient MSS by giving the full name. See also footnotes in the Zondervan TNIV Study Bible.

[6] See David N. Marshall, 'The Risen Jesus' in *The Essential Jesus: The Man, His Message, His Mission*, eds. B. W. Ball and W. G. Johnsson (Boise, Idaho: Pacific Press, 2002), pp. 180-191.

[7] G. O'Collins, *Contemporary Christian Insights: Interpreting Jesus* (London: Mowbray, 1983), p. 115; Michael Green, *The Empty Cross of Jesus* (London: Hodder & Stoughton, 1984), p. 102.

[8] Luke 24:11, TNIV.

[9] Luke 24:19-21, TNIV. N.B. the verb tenses.

[10] Luke 24:33-37, TNIV.

[11] John 20:3-9.

[12] Luke 24:12, MGE. See Luke 24:10-12 and John 20:1-9, 12.

[13] John 20:10, NLT.

[14] Mark 16:13, NLT.

[15] Luke 24:38, 39.

[16] Luke 24:27.

[17] Luke 24:37-43.

[18] Luke 24:44-49.

[19] John 20:25, NLT.

[20] John 11:16; 20:19 et seq.

[21] John 14:1-11.

[22] John 11:16.

[23] John 20:28.

[24] John 20:30, 31.

Chapter 22

. . . Risen Indeed!

When Thomas said, *'My Lord and my God!'* he showed that he understood as well as believed. And understanding *is* important.

The agonies of doubt behind him, Thomas believed and understood. And so may we.

At some level we all have a choice: to build on our faith or build on our doubts. The best way to build faith is in communion with the Risen Christ through prayer.

But is it possible to have a rational basis to our faith? Was the Resurrection an historical event? Thomas saw and believed. Can we assess the evidence and, through our questions, arrive at a basis for belief?

To counter the apostles' assertion that Jesus rose bodily from the tomb, the scientific rationalist says, 'Just check it out. Watch what happens when people die.' He proceeds to demonstrate that those who die decay and, ultimately, merge with the earth around them. Essentially, he is saying: Jesus' resurrection could not have happened because it is not repeatable.

Knowing *Jesus* Knowing **God**

However, miracles are, by definition, unprecedented events. Hence it is not logically valid to use science as an argument against them. We do not have an infallible knowledge of natural law, so we cannot exclude from the outset every possibility of unique events.

The case against a miracle is only acceptable when every report of that miracle has been investigated and found to be false. Such investigation is what we historians – Thomases all! – do! But we cannot adjudicate upon what history may or may not contain. Our job is to investigate the primary sources objectively and to report accordingly. In other words, to examine the testimonies of witnesses and the reliability of all the sources.

Among the earliest sources on the Resurrection, Paul's first letter to the Corinthian Christians was written in AD 54. The importance as a primary source of the fifteenth chapter of the first letter to the Corinthians is hard to exaggerate. In the first half-dozen verses Paul is quoting a much earlier source that had its origins among the apostles in the earliest post-Resurrection period.[1]

The post-Resurrection fragment is the generally accepted statement of Resurrection eyewitnesses. Peter is listed first, and also James. Then come the risen Christ's appearances to the disciple groups and His appearance 'to more than five hundred of the brothers and sisters at the same time, most of whom are still living'[2] and, hence, available for interview.

To a professional historian, the importance of that statement is huge.

It comes from a letter which the most authoritative scholars authenticate as a genuine letter written by someone in close touch with other eyewitnesses less than twenty-five years after the event. Few, if any, ancient events are supported by such early and sound evidence.

Three of the narrative accounts of the Resurrection (Matthew 28; Mark 16; Luke 24) were written from eyewitness accounts in the years between Paul's first letter to the Corinthians (AD 54) and the

... Risen Indeed!

fall of Jerusalem (AD 70). The fourth narrative account (John 20) was an eyewitness account, too, but written in Ephesus at the end of the first century.

Among the four accounts, there are the variations of detail inevitable in eyewitness accounts. These suggest an absence of collusion.

In his Resurrection account to the Corinthians, Paul set out his evidence in lawyer-like fashion, and, aware that a woman's testimony was not valid in a court of law, excluded the witness of the women. The authors of the four narrative accounts gave themselves no such constraints. The earliest witnesses on Resurrection Sunday *were* women. Hence their testimonies were included, regardless of considerations of legal plausibility. That was how it happened, so that was how it was set down.

Had first-century people set out to invent the Resurrection account they would not have invented it like this!

Jesus appeared to groups of varying sizes (between two and 500) and did so over a period of forty days. What they saw and experienced made heroes out of the men who had run from the scene of Jesus' arrest. The disciple who had three times denied knowing Jesus late on the night of the arrest became, post-Resurrection, the strongest and most defiant of the disciple band.[3] His transformation was typical of the others.

The empty tomb was Exhibit A when, at and after Pentecost, the disciples brought thousands of Jews – including many priests – to belief in the truth of the resurrection.

From Easter Sunday on, all the efforts of the Jewish establishment were meant to suppress reports of what had happened. But the word of the local and valorous disciples that God raised Jesus from the dead in vindication of His divinity was accepted by thousands. The tomb was empty. No one could say otherwise, so no one did. If the religious authorities believed the story they bribed the soldiers to tell – that the disciples had stolen

Knowing Jesus Knowing *God*

the body while they slept[4] – why was no attempt made to find and produce the body?

Instead, knowing that something supernatural had happened, the men of authority were unnerved, and bent their efforts – fruitlessly – to keeping a lid on the story.

Belief in the Resurrection did not arise because the disciples were expecting one. Far from it. Further, an objective encounter of the disciples with the risen Jesus is the only way we can explain their subsequent behaviour and, as a result, the growth of the Church. Visions and subjective experiences would not have done it. These men were imprisoned, tortured and killed in all manner of grisly ways. They would not have done that in defence of a lie. 'I have seen the Lord!' they exclaimed.

The risen Lord had *spoken* to them and *walked* with them. He had *distributed food* to them and *eaten* with them. He had *blessed them* and *touched them* with nail-pierced hands.[5]

Jesus of Nazareth did not only die. He rose to a new, an endless life, which enables you to meet Him. He is still able to transform lives as He did in the first century.

Jesus is not someone who *was*. He is Somebody who *is*, and who offers faith to doubters, and answers to those who question.

John R. W. Stott said, 'Christianity is in its very essence a resurrection faith. The concept of resurrection lies at its heart.'

Under the persecution of authoritarian regimes from the first to the twenty-first centuries, Christians have identified themselves by saying, 'He is risen!', provoking the response, 'Risen indeed!'

[1] Michael Green, op cit, pp. 96, 97.
[2] 1 Corinthians 15:6, TNIV.
[3] See Acts 4:8-12.
[4] Matthew 28:11-15.
[5] Matthew 28:1, 7, 9, 18-20; Luke 24:13-16, 30, 34, 39-46, 50; John 20:14, 18, 20, 30; Acts 1:3, 4; 1 Corinthians 15:5-8.

Conclusion

There's a Choice

Jesus is not just a figure among many in the pantheon of world religions. He stands tall and stands out to such an extent that it becomes clear that Jesus does not belong there.

Why?

Jesus is alive. He is God. The goal of the Christian faith is that we should not just encounter Jesus, but know Him, and form a strong, personal relationship with Him. Jesus comes to us, cares about all aspects of our life, and wants to become the centre around which our life is built. As we commit to Him we enter the experience called 'salvation' or 'justification' which we have explained in this book. Through that experience we receive the assurance of the eternal life won for us by Christ's conquest of death.

Eternal life is the goal of the disciple of Christ. And He calls *you* to be His disciple. Eternal life is emphatically *not* an endless period in which we work off our karma (guilt) or an indefinite number of reincarnations. Our guilt is dealt with as we accept

Knowing *Jesus* Knowing *God*

justification through faith in Jesus' death on our behalf. Our battle with sin goes on – but, as we fight it, we have a shield against the assaults of evil, and a Captain who has never lost a battle.

We need to know the Father God through His perfect revelation in Jesus, and through the daily, hourly interventionist help He provides through the Holy Spirit.

In God there is no unChristlikeness, and never has been. We come to know Him through the four Gospels, by far the easiest portions of the Bible to understand. These Gospels are the *lenses* through which we view the God revealed throughout Scripture. Knowing Jesus is knowing God. And we come to know Him, first, through the four Gospels.

Communication is the key to the success of any relationship. Communication with God is:

- Through prayer;
- Through prayerful and daily exposure to His Word (that includes daily exposure to the life of Jesus, in addition to any other study or reading you may be doing);
- Through seeking the solution to the sin problem through Jesus, along the lines outlined in chapters 16 and onwards (a part of this book that ideally should be studied, as well as read);
- Finally, through exposure to God through worship.

Christians are sometimes said to worship their work, work at their play, and play at their worship. We cannot afford to play at our worship. Worship must involve a personal encounter with God.

Worship usually involves participation in a corporate worship experience. Corporate worship is meant to magnify God and give us an up-close-and-personal experience with Him.

A recent worship survey of Bible-belt Christians in the southern states of America revealed that as many as two-thirds of respondents reported that they had 'never' experienced the close

Conclusion: There's a Choice

presence of God in a church service. Clearly there has been something wrong. Institutional Christianity – Walter Martin and C. S. Lewis called it 'churchianity' – has been experienced as a mixed blessing. Christian journalist Philip Yancey has told the story of his escape from 'churchianity' in his many books and on YouTube.

Institutional churches are apt to be the purveyors of what we have called 'religion' as opposed to the Gospel and the Person of Christ. Religion can be a toxic mix in which politics and economics predominate over faith and things of the Spirit. In chapters 6-10 we described the campaign of Jesus against the religion of His day. We said that Jesus came to replace religion with Himself. Too often, religion is part of the problem. We stressed that the Gospel of Jesus Christ is *not* a religion.

Forms, rules, rituals and hierarchies are the paraphernalia of religion. These can detract from – certainly *dis*tract from – the worship of God.

Hence, as we choose a faith community with which to identify and with whom to worship, we choose with some care. We look for a community where Christ is uplifted, the close presence of God is felt in worship, and the Bible is believed as the only basis for faith and lifestyle.

As we grow in our knowledge of, and relationship with, Jesus through prayer, prayerful study and worship, we grow spiritually. We adventure. We encounter the God who both rages and weeps at the injustices of our world. And, more than that, He promises the ultimate triumph of right and justice, the death of death, the termination of the terminator, and the establishment of God's Kingdom.

Finally, we are lost in ourselves until we admit that we are flawed human beings, sinners.

The fundamental difference between Christianity and religion is

Knowing *Jesus* Knowing *God*

that religions tell us to seek salvation in a radically different way than the way described in the Gospel of Jesus. Other major religions were founded by teachers who show us the way to salvation. Only Jesus claims to *be* the Way of Salvation Himself.

The miracle at the heart of Christianity still works when we embrace the Good News of Jesus. Once we do that, *we* become a part of the Jesus narrative just as Jesus becomes a part of us.

Roman executioners were professional killers who never let rebel leaders slip from their clutches. Jesus, three days after being rendered thoroughly dead by a Roman execution squad, was found to be very thoroughly and very bodily alive again. The resurrected Jesus became the first of a new creation. He invites you, too, to be part of that new creation. That way, with Him, you become light in an increasingly dark and uncertain world.